LAS ANIMAS, HUERFANO AND CUSTER:

THREE COLORADO COUNTIES ON A CULTURAL FRONTIER

A HISTORY OF THE RATON BASIN

By Robert A. Murray

Colorado State Office
Bureau of Land Management
Denver, Colorado
1978

FOREWORD

This document presents the sixth volume in a series of cultural resource reports. The study concerns historic sites and values on public lands in Colorado. It was originally derived from a contract that was awarded to Western Interpretive Services as an integral part of the Bureau of Land Management's Cultural Resources Management Program.

A major objective of the Bureau of Land Management, Department of the Interior is the preservation of the nation's historic heritage and values, particularly those under the jurisdiction of the Bureau.

The history of Raton Basin was originally designed to provide a base-line narrative for planning and environmental purposes. Robert A. Murray has written a new history of these three counties and it will become a part of an overall history of the Canon City, Colorado District. As the histories for the balance of the eastern slope are written, they will be made available to the public.

It is my pleasure to make this latest volume of the Cultural Resources Series available to the public and to the professional community.

DALE R. ANDRUS
State Director, Colorado
Bureau of Land Management

TABLE OF CONTENTS

ILLUSTRATIONS

MAPS

ACKNOWLEDGMENTS

This project is prepared as a Cultural Resource Overview (History), under the terms of Contract #CO-910-CT7-2547, awarded to Western Interpretive Services on September 30, 1977.

Beginning with work in WIS's extensive files and accessible library sources, a background file was set up on the historic context of the Raton Basin as defined in the contract. Then WIS set out to visit major sources in Colorado.

The most important blocks of material were found at the Western History Collections, Denver Public Library; at the State Historical Society of Colorado and in the Western History Research Collections of the Pueblo, Colorado Regional Library. There is a limited amount of locally significant material, mostly clipping-scrapbooks, at the Trinidad Public Library. A little material on specialized topics and localities was found at the Western History Department of the Public Library and at the Pioneer Museum in Colorado Springs. Materials at the University of Colorado in Boulder appear limited to specialized collections on railroads and coal-mining activities of Colorado Fuel and Iron Company.

Dr. Morris Taylor of Trinidad Junior College, Joanne Dodds of the Pueblo Library, and the reference staffs Denver Public Library and at the State Historical Society were all cooperative in the location of special source materials. Dr. Frederic Athearn, State Historian, BLM, Colorado, proved helpful throughout the project.

INTRODUCTION

The Raton Basin, which consists of three southeastern Colorado
counties, is a unique land in which early European settlement occurred;
long before most other parts of Colorado. Not only did plains natives
such as the Comanche, Ute, and Apache roam the hills and valleys of the
region, but Spanish explorers and military expeditions ventured out of
the San Luis Valley or over Raton Pass in order to chase Indians or to
trade with them. From the 1690s to the early nineteenth century there
were a few Spanish visitors including Juan Bautisa de Anza, the tamer
of the Comanche.

During the nineteenth century the land was both American and Spanish.
From the time of Zebulon Pike's expedition into the area through the
exploits of Steven Long, the Americans saw the region as theirs. The
Spanish, and after 1821, the Mexicans, disputed this and did their best
to protect this isolated outpost of the Mexican frontier. The Spanish
built a fort near Sangre de Cristo Pass in 1819 and after that was
abandoned, so was much of the Raton Basin. American fur trappers and
traders made their way into the basin during the 1820s and 1830s. The
establishment of the Northern Cutoff of the Santa Fe Trail caused further
development including a settlement near present-day Pueblo, called
Milk Fort.

The Mexican government decided in the 1840s to prevent American
incursions into southern Colorado and northern New Mexico by settling the
land. To this end, grants of millions of acres of land were made to
Mexican citizens if they promised to settle the grants. The Maxwell Grant,

the Vigil Grant, and others were made and here is where the first small settlements arose.

Settlement by the Mexican government ended in 1848 when the Mexican War came to a conclusion. With the defeat of Mexico, the United States gained clear title to the rest of Colorado and most of the western United States as we know it. American settlers began to filter into the Raton Basin and by 1865 a range cattle industry had developed.

Cattlemen put their herds out on Public Domain and fenced off the range. Anglo and Spanish cattle ranchers came to view the lands along the rivers as theirs by prior right.

In the 1870s the Denver and Rio Grande Western Railroad and the Atchison, Topeka and Santa Fe Railroad both reached Trinidad and the Raton Basin boomed. Coal mining became a major industry by 1880, supplying the steel works at Pueblo, Colorado. At the same time, the Wet Mountain Valley saw its first development.

In 1870 Carl Wulsten brought in about 350 people to the Wet Mountain Valley and the settlement of Colfax was created. This little community was primarily German in origin; and by 1875 it had broken up. The next movement into the Wet Mountain Valley came in the late 1870s when silver was discovered. Querida, Rosita, Silver Cliff, Westcliffe were all founded at this time. The silver boom lasted into the 1890s and then the valley became primarily agricultural with Westcliffe as the main population center.

The area around Walsenburg and Trinidad became, by 1890, the state's most important coal producing region. The importation of foreign workers caused the two towns to develop strong ethnic communities. There were

Italians, Serbs, Slavs, and so forth along with the native Spanish-speaking population. This mixture of cultures caused tension and discontent that culminated in a series of strikes against the mine owners.

In 1903 a major coal strike united the various ethnic groups for the first time and from then on, through Ludlow Massacre of 1914 the miners were united against the principal mine owners, mainly Colorado Fuel and Iron of Pueblo. By the early 1920s coal mining was being mechanized and coal production was dropping. Many miners left the area and agriculture became the mainstay of the region's economy.

Cattle ranching, alfalfa raising, wheat farming, and some coal production stayed the economy during the 1920s and 1930s. The advent of major highways brought tourists into the area during the 1930s and today the economy of the Raton Basin remains little unchanged from forty years ago.

In his work, Robert A. Murray has presented, for the first time, a consolidated history of these three counties. The reader will note that it is a general work and does not attempt original research. Rather, this document will provide the reader a solid background for the history of the Raton Basin.

Frederic J. Athearn
Denver, Colorado 1978

Chapter I. BACKGROUND AND SETTING

This part of Colorado lay millions of years ago, on the margins of vast, but shallow seas. Here, extensive deposits of erosional debris from nearby lands built up. Subsequently these consolidated into layers of sedimentary rock, the shales, sandstones and the coal deposits of today's region.

Some 60,000,000 years ago there began a new and greater uplifting of the land out of shallow seas. A sequence of uplifts, the Laramide Revolution, ushered in a mountain-building process that may still be going on. While this continued, the forces of erosion stripped away vast areas of material from the higher slopes and laid down newer sedimentary deposits in a broad plain at the foot of the rising mountain range. Further uplifting, folding and faulting began to produce the outlines of mountain ranges of recognizeable form.

More erosion shaped the ranges, filled intervening valleys with sediments, and in some circumstances carved canyons deep into the rock and washed boulders and gravel clear down to the lower stream courses at the edge of the plains. As time went on, the streams cut deeply into the uptilted western edge of the plains and dissected the intervening terrain into mesas, buttes and other rough landforms.[1]

The uplifting of the Sangre de Cristo and of other ranges farther west cut off moist Pacific air from the region. Now only the low pressure areas of major storms, or the monsoon-effect of summer could bring moist air this far inland from the Gulf. At lower elevations summer thundershowers brought most of the useful moisture. Farther up slope, added cooling of the higher elevation extracts more moisture from the air over a longer season.

2

The overall effect is a semiarid climate with short winters and long summers. Local microclimates of the foothills country provide the most comfortable wintering locations for animals and for man.[2]

The lowland areas of this region are covered with a short grass turf, with buffalo grass predominating in historic times. On the rough lands, soil conditions and patterns of run-off and retention of moisture create a more varied pattern. There small, brushy trees like piñon pine, scrub oak and juniper cover large areas.

Only on the higher slopes is there sufficient moisture and cool enough temperatures to support a growth of pine and other types of evergreens.[3]

In the earliest times of consequence to man, there were wildlife species now no longer present, such as the Columbian mammoth and several types of large, long-horned bison. But for most of late prehistoric and historic times, this area has had about the same pattern of wildlife resources that the explorers found and that the pioneers utilized for subsistence.

Bison ranged over the plains and into the mountain valleys. Elk summered in the mountains and poured down to winter in the more salubrious foothills climate. Bighorn sheep used the brush lands of the rough breaks, buttes and mesas. On the plains, the teeming herds of bison were joined by great herds of antelope. There were modest numbers of beaver and small fur-bearers in the woods and along the streams. Predators ranging from the fearsome plains-grizzly bear down through the little kit-fox and the black-footed ferret were found wherever their prey might be during a given season.

Turkeys used the piñon forests. Several species of grouse ranged at different elevations. A host of colorful songbirds frequented the area. And eagles, hawks, owls and scavenging vultures soared overhead.[4]

Into this setting at some time in the distant past came man. Scattered and frail evidence suggests he may have come as long as 20 to 50,000 years ago.[5]

The early hunters of large game in the period six to fifteen thousand years ago were better understood through archeological evidence. Skilled workmen with definite stylistic traditions, they left behind an abundance of stone tools. In many cases, these have been found in direct association with game kills.[6]

Then for about 3,000 years a drier climate prevailed here. People had less game to harvest and came to depend more upon the berries, seeds and roots to supplement hunting opportunities.[7]

Soon new settlers arrived in the desert valleys of what is now northern New Mexico and southwestern Colorado. The newcomers were well-organized town-dwellers, dependent upon irrigated farming for their subsistence. Despite several thousand years of cultural change along with various relocations, the Pueblo Indians still survive as distinct cultural groups in nearby New Mexico. Through amalgamation with later Latin and Anglo population groups some of their people became important infusion to the mixed-blood population of the Raton Basin.[8]

For several thousand years the Raton Basin was a frontier region between the urbanized pueblo dwellers in New Mexico and the more primitive hunting tribes like the Apaches and Utes. The pueblo tribes regarded the Huatollas (today called the Spanish Peaks) as frontier landmarks, setting off their territory from that of the wild tribes to the northeast.

4

When the first Spanish explorers came over the passes from New Mexico in the 1500's, they found the hunting tribes wandering on foot over the plains, living in small skin tipis, and packing their belongings about on dogs while they searched for far-ranging bison. The tribes on the plains in our immediate area of interest at this point were Apaches, who had probably come into the area from the north about 300 years earlier.

These Apaches centered their economy around the bison, but like most primitive tribes, extracted nearly all their other needs from the environment of the region. By the beginning of the Spanish contact period they had begun to use some surplus dried meat, rawhide, hide robes and a few other items for trade at the Pueblo settlements such as Taos. In exchange they received corn, fiber products and portable handicraft items.[9]

As the Spanish tightened their religious and political hold over New Mexico, the Apaches on the Plains and the Utes in the mountain parks made a dramatic change in their own way of life. Acquiring horses from the Spanish settlements through trade and raiding, they increased the range over which they could hunt and raid. They could now carry more trade goods and more loot. Consequently the pace of both trade and warefare picked up briskly.

The Apaches began to raid more settled tribes on the rivers of the central plains, like the Wichitas and Caddoes. From those settlements they carried slaves to trade off in New Mexico. They raided the fringes of the Spanish settlements for horses and for captives to be held for ransom. From about 1650 to 1725 they dominated a wide area.[10]

Then a dramatic change took place. A branch of the Snake Indians, as well supplied with horses as the Apaches, pushed down into the plains along the North Platte Valley. They made contact with French traders who operated out of bases on the Mississippi, and obtained guns and ammunition from them. Thus armed, these Comanches pushed southward into the Apache country. At the same time the tribes on the eastern fringe of the plains also became better armed.

Now the Apaches were the prey, and through the mid-1700's many Apache captives were traded east to be shipped down the Mississippi and off to the islands of the Caribbean. Apache remnants were crowded off the plains into the mountains and deserts of New Mexico and Arizona, where they remained a perpetual problem for the Spanish settlers for another hundred years.[11]

NOTES ON CHAPTER I

1. E. N. Goddard and T. S. Lovering, *Geology and Ore Deposits of the Front Range, Colorado*, (Washington, D.C.: U.S. Geological Survey, 1950).

   R. F. Flint, *Glacial and Pleistocene Geology*, (New York: John Wiley & Sons, 1957).

   R. C. Hills, *Spanish Peaks, Colorado, Geologic Folio*, (Washington, D.C.: U.S. Geological Survey, 1901).

   _____. *Walsenburg, Colorado, Geologic Folio*, (Washington, D.C.: U.S. Geological Survey, 1900).

2. U.S. Department of Agriculture, *Climate and Man, The 1941 Yearbook of Agriculture*, (Washington, D.C.: Government Printing Office, 1941), pp. 798-808.

3. W. A. Dayton, *et. al*, *Range Plant Handbook*, (Washington, D.C.: U.S. Department of Agriculture, 1937).

   William A. Weber, "Plant Geography in the Southern Rocky Mountains," in *The Quaternary of the United States*, (H.E. Wright, Jr. and G. Frey, eds), (Princeton, N.J.: Princeton University Press, 1965.), pp. 453-468.

4. Josiah Gregg, *Commerce of the Prairies*, (Philadelphia: Lippincott, 1962), Vol. 2, pp. 287-302.

   Edwin James, *Account of An Expedition from Pittsburgh to the Rocky Mountains...*, (Philadelphia: Carey & Lea, 1823), Vol. 1, pp. 458-503 and Vol. 2, pp. 22-40 and 45-57.

5. Kenneth MacGowan and Joseph A. Hester, Jr., *Early Man in the New World*, (N.Y.: Doubleday, 1962), pp.

6. George A. Agogino, "The Paleo Indian in North America," *Genus*, Vol. 19, #1-4 (1963), pp. 3-17.

7. Waldo R. Wedel, "Some Aspects of Human Ecology in the Central Plains," *American Anthropologist*, Vol.55 (1953), pp. 499-514.

8. E. B. Renaud, "The Indians of Colorado," in: *Colorado: Short Studies of its Past and Present*, (Boulder: University of Colorado, 1927).

9. George E. Hyde, *Indians of the High Plains*, (Norman: University of Oklahoma Press, 1959), pp. 26-29.

10. Frank R. Secoy, *Changing Military Patterns on the Great Plains*, (Locust Valley, N.Y.: J.J. Augustin, 1953.). pp. 16 ff.

11. Hyde, *op.cit.*, pp. 115 ff.

Chapter II. A COLONIAL FRONTIER

The three counties of Raton Basin saw little Spanish activity for all their general dominance over the region. The Coronado expedition on the plains in 1541 bypassed southeastern Colorado by a wide margin. Most subsequent Spanish activity for many years concentrated on the subjection of the inhabitants of the pueblos of the lower Rio Grande Valley, on the Pecos and elsewhere in New Mexico, and on exploratory visits to the wandering tribes of the plains in eastern New Mexico and Texas.

One party is associated with the Raton Basin. This was the expedition of Captain Francisco Leyva de Bonilla. He led a rebellious force of Spanish soldiers who broke off from an official expedition to one of the New Mexico villages. They wintered at San Idelfonso in 1593-94. After visiting Pecos Pueblo in 1594, they pushed off into the plains.

While among the Wichitas, along the Arkansas River (probably well to the east of the Colorado line), further trouble broke out and Antonio Gutierrez de Humana killed Bonilla. The rebels then ranged north as far as the Kansas River and back to the country of the Wichitas. At some point on the return trip, they were set upon by Wichita Indians, and most of the soldiers killed.

These rebels traveling without priests have given rise to the name for one of the tributaries of the Arkansas: the Rio de Las Animas Perdidas en Purgatorio, variously spelled, pronounced and translated, but all meaning today's Purgatory River, one of the main Arkansas tributaries that drains a good deal of the Raton Basin.[1]

The expeditions of Zaldivar in 1598 and of Oñate in 1599-1601 also missed this area on their trips onto the plains.[2]

Revolting against Spanish rule in 1639, the people of Taos Pueblo abandoned their homes and trailed out over the plains to join Apache bands they knew in western Kansas. Here, they built the pueblo of El Cuartelejo in present Scott County. By the 1660's they had all returned to Taos.[3]

The Pueblo Revolt in the summer of 1680 had little effect north of New Mexico execpt to restore direct long-standing trade relationships between the Apaches and the Pueblo tribes for a time. Over the years 1693-1696, the Spanish reconquered the province. During this conflict, the Picuris fled to El Cuartelejo for a short stay.[4]

In the early 1700's French traders operating from bases along the Mississippi River began to markedly influence events on the plains by providing trade goods and arms to the Osages, Missouris and Kansas Indians with whom the Apache were at war.[5]

By this same time, the northernmost pueblos and their Apache allies found themselves under continued pressure from the Comanche, the Pawnee and their allies. In 1706, Captain Juan de Ulibarri was commissioned to command a reconaissance mission to reenforce the now-friendly Apaches and to ascertain the extent of French influence on the plains. Ulibarri, warned of a possible ambush on Raton Pass, took a circuitous route through the hills, crossed most of the southern tributaries of the Arkansas River, and in August of 1706 reached the Arkansas River near the present site of Pueblo, Colorado. En route he conferred with several different bands of Apaches and with the Picuris who were visiting them.[6]

Some of the Apaches, notably those the Spanish called the Faraon (Pharoah), continued to be troublesome on the New Mexican frontier. In 1715, the governor, Juan Ignacio Flores Mogollon, led an expedition against them on the plains without decisive result.

In 1717, a new governor ad interim, Antonio Valverde, led the largest expedition yet assembled out onto the plains of eastern New Mexico, this time in support of the Apaches against the troublesome Comanche. Hearing rumors of approaching French troops, Valverde withdrew that fall to Santa Fe without making contact with an active enemy.[8] Two years later, Valverde sent Captain Pedro Villasur on a far-reaching expedition against the allies of the now-feared French. Villasur reached a point near the forks of the Platte in present Nebraska, when on August 14 of 1719 his camp was overrun by the Pawnees. Spanish losses were heavy and only a handful of stragglers trickled into Santa Fe to report the disaster.[9]

Internal problems plagued the northern Spanish provinces over the next half-century and practically excluded effective Spanish military operations on the northeastern frontier.[10]

As the 18th Century wore on, Comanche raiders became increasingly active on the frontier of New Mexico. In contrast to the Apaches, they established alliances and trade connections on their eastern range. Here the resident tribes were often visited by far ranging small trading parties out of the French settlements on the Mississippi. The combination of mobility with the latest weapons made the Comanche a formidable adversary.[11]

At this same time, some of the Apaches were still active as raiders in eastern New Mexico. Others of this people extended their raids across the Rio Grande into other parts of the province. Spanish strategy called for the Comanche to become allies against the Apaches.

New Mexico Governor Juan Bautista de Anza set out to do just this in the fall of 1779. He assembled a force of over 600 soldiers, miliamen and Pueblo Indian allies. Moving out of New Mexico on a course up the Rio Grande Valley, de Anza's column came into the Raton Basin over Sangre de Cristo Pass, and descended into the foothills into the heart of the Comanche range.

De Anza caught a major Comanche camp unguarded, with its fighting men away on a raid. Taking advantage of this situation, the Spanish force destroyed the encampment and then laid an ambush on what we now call Greenhorn Creek for the returning war party.

The trap worked, and de Anza inflicted numerous casualties on the Comanche force. Among the dead was Cuerno Verde, a principal chief, so called because of the green-painted buffalo horns of his headdress.[12]

De Anza alternated military shows-of-force with peace overtures. By so doing, he maneuvered the Comanche tribes into a lasting truce that contributed to the final downfall of the Apaches on the plains.[13] The truce also paved the way for trade between the New Mexicans and the Comanche and a specialized commerce grew up. The Indians brought in not only dried meat and hides, but significant numbers of Apache prisoners and numerous horses for sale at the New Mexico settlements. Traders who went out on the prairie to deal with the Indians became known as "Comancheros". They were an important factor in the logistic support of Comanche raiders until the mid-1870's.[14]

With an effective flow of trade goods available from the east and the west, the Comanche tribesmen became the most powerful and affluent force of Indians in the Southern Plains. They drove most of the remaining Apaches from the plains. They raided the settlements of other tribes in Texas.[15]

While this was going on, international affairs played a part in shaping the history of the region. At the close of the Seven Years War in 1763, Britain and Spain dismantled the North American colonies of France. Spain received the province of Louisiana, which in effect was the country drained by the western tributaries of the Mississippi, north of the older Spanish possessions.

While Spain administered the external affairs of Louisiana out of a headquarters in New Orleans, its hold was sufficiently loose to permit a continuation of the Indain trade by the independent French frontiersmen.[16]

The Comanches, now at the height of their power, kept up their trade with both the Comancheros and the French residents of Louisiana's settlements on the lower Missouri River. They began to push their raids farther into Texas, and ultimately deep into the interior of northern Mexico. This three-way relationship between the Comanches and the residents and administrators of the Spanish territories created a complex set of problems.

The Spanish officials continued to respond on a localized basis while changing policy at the higher levels made it impossible to really bring the Comanches under control through coordinated action.[17]

Then, the French Revolution shook western Europe and brought on new international conflicts during which Napoleon Bonaparte became in effect the dictator of a new French empire. Napoleon needed money with which to support his armies. To get it, he coerced Spain into returning Louisiana to France so that he might sell it to the United States.

The official ceremonies of transfer in New Orleans and in St. Louis in 1803 ushered in a period of change for the region. No longer was Louisiana a buffer between the older Spanish territories and the U.S. Instead, a prime area for the expansion of U.S. trade and opened a new frontier for American settlers.[18]

Having acquired the territory, President Thomas Jefferson sent out several expeditions to determine first hand its extent and its potential resources. In 1804-1806, the Lewis and Clark Expedition pushed up the Missouri and over into the Columbia Basin.[19] Other expeditions probed the southeastern part of the new territory.[20]

Then, in 1806, came an American expedition of much greater concern to officials of the shaky Spanish colonial administration. French and Spanish versions of the southwestern boundary of Louisiana differed sharply. France held that the boundary was formed by the Red River of the South clear to its headwaters. The Americans hoped they would find that point in the main ranges of the Southern Rockies. The army sent Lieutenant Zebulon M. Pike into the region to find out.[21]

Pike's small force pushed out across the prairies of Kansas and moved up the Arkansas River. They sighted the Rockies on the the 15th of November, 1806. Near the site of Pueblo they built a small defensive bastion. Then they began to search for the headwaters of Red River, which Pike believed must be in the high mountains nearby. All of the streams they reconnoitred turned out to be tributaries of the Arkansas.[22]

From the foothills near present Canon City, they prepared for one more try toward the southwest in search of the Red River. They moved up Grape Creek and into the Raton Basin, and found the Wet Mountain Valley, at this season a frozen hell for men in summer clothes. The party pushed on over Sangre de Cristo and Medano passes into the upper Rio Grande Valley. Here they built a small stockade. Surprised by Spanish troops, the members of the expedition were disarmed, and taken deep into Mexico for questioning. They lost to their captors their maps, notes and most other papers. Pike managed to retain his diary, and the members of the expedition were able to reconstruct from their memories a fairly coherent picture of the country they traversed.[23]

The next official expedition to reach the area was that of Major Stephen H. Long, an Army engineer, in the summer of 1820. Ranging out across the prairies, they passed southward along the foot of the Front Range to the north bank of the Arkansas. Opposite the mouth of the Huerfano River, they split their force. Long, with one contingent, crossed the Arkansas near present Timpas Creek and headed southeast across the Purgatory and Chacuaco Creek to the crest of the Mesa de Maya and went down the Cimmaron to the Arkansas. The other party went down the Arkansas and they both moved on east to return to the States.[24]

The primary impact of the Pike and Long expeditions was to publicize the relative ease of travel over the plains and to show that there were several routes that gave access to the Spanish settlements of New Mexico. Along with the expeditions of several private traders, they drew attention to the potential for trade with that region.

Spanish reactions to these moves demonstrated that colonial officials were justifiably disturbed over the long range intentions of U.S.
citizens and their government. They felt that trade restrictions might
impede the development of American interests in the territory. So,
Robert McKnight landed in Spanish jail in 1812. Auguste Choteau and
Jules de Mun came up the Arkansas in 1815 and pushed up the Huerfano
River over Sangre de Cristo Pass and down into Taos, where Spanish
officials confiscated their pack train and its cargo. Undaunted by
this, the partners brought out another trading expedition and ran into
further problems in 1817.[25]

Disturbed by free-traders on the one hand, and by rumors occasioned
by the assembly of the Atkinson Expedition on the Missouri, Governor
Facundo Melgares built a small fort along the course of South Oak Creek
to guard Sangre de Cristo Pass in 1819. This was soon overrun or abandoned to the Comanches who ranged the area.[26]

Late in August of 1821, the Mexicans overthrew Spanish rule. In
New Mexico, this meant that imperial policy considerations could no
longer interfere with the popular demand for trade with the Americans.
At the first celebration of independence in January of 1822, Melgares
announced that American traders would be admitted to the territory.
William Becknell, a trader from Missouri, was already there.[27] Others
soon followed.

Jacob Fowler, with a party of traders and trappers came in to Taos
in the fall of 1822, traveling up the Huerfano River and South Oak
Creek, past the abandoned Spanish fort.[28]

The pioneering traders carried back not only word of substantial welcome in the Mexican settlements, but substantial profits from their venture. Their work ushered in a new era in frontier relationships in which the traders played a dominant role.

NOTES ON CHAPTER II

1. Jack D. Forbes, *Apache, Navaho and Spaniard*, (Norman: University of Oklahoma Press, 1960), pp. 74-76.

2. George P. Hammond and Agapito Rey (eds. & trans.), *Don Juan de Onate, Colonizer of New Mexico, 1595-1628*, (Albuquerque: University of New Mexico Press, 1953), Vol. 1, pp. 215-228.

3. Ralph E. Twitchell (comp.) *The Spanish Archives of New Mexico*, (Cedar Rapids: Torch Press, 1914), Vol. 2, pp. 279-280.

4. Forbes, *op. cit.*, p. 271.

5. Hyde, *op. cit.*, pp. 146-148.

6. *ibid.*, pp. 64-68.

7. A. B. Thomas, *Plains Indians and New Mexico*, (Albuquerque, University of New Mexico, 1940), pp. 8-18.

8. A. B. Thomas, *After Coronado, Spanish Exploration Northeast of New Mexico, 1696-1727*, (Norman: University of Oklahoma Press, 1935), pp. 134-137.

9. *ibid.* p. 135.

10. Hyde, *op. cit.*, pp. 95-115.

11. Hyde, *ibid.* pp. 115 ff.

12. T. R. Fehrenbach, *Comanches, The Destruction of a People*, (N.Y., Knopf, 1974), pp. 221-226.

13. Hyde, *op. cit.*, pp. 162-168.

14. J. Evertts Haley, "The Comanchero Trade," *Southwestern Historical Quarterly*, Vol. 38 (1934-35), pp. 157-176.

15. Fehrenbach, *op. cit.*, pp. 169-180.

16. John Keats, *Eminent Domain, The Louisiana Purchase and The Making of America*, (N.Y.: Charterhouse, 1973), pp. 170-173 and pp. 215-223.

    also:

    letter, Estevan Miro to Alange, August 7, 1792, quoted in Abraham P. Nasatir, *Before Lewis and Clark*, (St. Louis: St. Louis Historical Documents Foundation, 1952), Vol. 1, pp. 157-160.

17. Fehrenbach, *op. cit.*, pp. 226 ff.

18. Keats, *op. cit.*, pp. 302-339.

19. John B. Brebner, *The Explorers of North America, 1492-1806,* (N.Y.: Doubleday, 1955), pp. 383-403.

20. Isaac J. Cox, "The Exploration of the Louisiana Frontier, 1803-1806," *American Historical Review* (Annual Report for 1904), pp. 152 ff.

21. Zebulon M. Pike, *Sources of the Mississippi and the Western Louisiana Territory,* (Ann Arbor, Michigan: University of Microfilms, 1966), pp. 107-110.

22. *ibid.*, pp. 111-188.

23. *ibid.*, p. 189 ff.

24. Edwin James (compiler), *Account of An Expedition from Pittsburgh to the Rocky Mountains...* (Philadelphia: Carey & Lee, 1823), Vol. 2, pp. 45-119 and pp. 458-503.

25. Marshall Sprague, *Great Gates,* (Boston: Little, Brown and Co. 1964), pp. 91-93.

26. Chauncey Thomas, "The Spanish Fort in Colorado, 1819," *Colorado Magazine,* Vol. 14, #3 (May, 1937), pp. 81-85.

27. F. F. Stevens, (ed.), "Missouri and the Santa Fe Trade," *Missouri Historical Review,* Vol. 10 (1915-1916), pp. 233-262.

28. Jacob Fowler (Elliott Coues, ed.), *The Journal of Jacob Fowler,* (N.Y.: F. P. Harper, 1898), pp. 1-10.

Chapter III. THE TRADERS' FRONTIER

The traders who followed in William Becknell's wake forged economic ties between the New Mexican settlements and the Missouri frontier that grew stronger year by year. The resources of the two areas complemented one another in such a way as to make the trade mutually profitable.

Textiles and small hardware were in the greatest demand in New Mexico. Mexican gold and silver were popular on the cash-short Missouri frontier, as were the cheap and plentiful horses, mules and other animals of New Mexico.[1]

Traders' caravans soon left a well-marked trail from Independence, Missouri, southwestward across the Kansas prairies to the Arkansas River. Early expeditions followed the Arkansas upstream to the mouth of Timpas Creek and turned up that stream for 25 miles before cutting across to the Purgatory River which they followed to Raton Pass. This "mountain branch" of the Santa Fe Trail ran through the Raton Basin in present Las Animas County for about 50 miles.[2]

William Becknell, seeking an easier gradient wagon route in 1822, pioneered the Cimarron Cut-Off, bypassing the rough country of Southern Colorado by traversing northeastern New Mexico about 60 miles to the southeast of Raton Pass. After that time, most heavy freight wagon traffic took the Becknell route. Pack trains sometimes used the "mountain branch," but it developed greater importance for trappers and traders who dealt with the Indians.[3]

By coincidence, 1822 marked the revival of interest on the part of Missouri businessmen in the fur resources of the Rockies. William H. Ashley and his associates set in motion a new phase of fur trade activity in the northern plains and Rockies between 1822 and 1824.[4]

World-wide, the trade in valuable small furs faced a number of problems. Manufacturers of felt hats were developing the technology to utilize cheaper furs. The French Revolution and the Napoleonic Wars had for twenty years and more severely disturbed the old patterns of trade between Britain and the Continent, and new trading channels were only now being developed across the revised national boundaries created by the Congress of Vienna.

Further, well-organized large scale fur trading operations in Canada offered sharp competition to the American fur industry. They could do this because they had access to the British manufactured goods the Indians preferred without the tariff barrier erected here to benefit American manufacturers.

But American furs found a major outlet in the China trade, where New England merchants had a sound foothold at this time.[5]

The Rockies looked attractive to American fur traders because the older fur country of the Ohio Valley and the lower Missouri River country were being overrun by settlement. For the next twenty years, merchants on the Missouri frontier experimented with a series of approaches to making the western fur trade a paying proposition.

From the first, they found that the Indians of the region did not really care for trapping beaver.[6] Then it became evident that populations of valuable fur animals were really thin in this region compared to their density in Canada and the older fur country around the Great Lakes. Beaver at climax population levels probably averaged about three to the mile on most mountain streams in the west.[7]

The Missouri traders recruited trappers from the young men of their own settlements. Some came from the long-established French families, like Ceran St. Vrain, Antoine Roubidoux, and others from the clusters of American backwoodsmen now crowding the frontier, like Tom Smith, Ewing Young, and William Bent. Soon called the "mountain men," at first they specialized in systematically trapping beaver. In the northern Rockies, for some years they disposed of their catch at annual rendezvous held by major fur trading partnerships. In the southern part of the beaver range, they often traded off their furs at places like Taos and Santa Fe.[8]

Many of these "mountain men" also ran small-scale trading ventures among the Indians of the regions they traveled. Most of them developed social connections with the Indian tribes or with the New Mexicans. Some of them, like Richens L.Wootten, Maurice LeDuc, Matthew Kinkead, Charles Autobees and William Bent, remained important in the region long after the peak of the fur trade days passed. All of them gained an intimate acquaintance of the plains and mountains in the course of their extensive travels.[9]

The trading companies that linked the trappers to the channels of world fur marketing encountered a number of problems. They fought high operating overhead and costly transportation for trade goods going west and furs moving east. They bought the British trade goods that the Indians and the trappers preferred, paying high prices, topped in some cases by import duties. They borrowed operating capital at interest rates that generally ranged upward from the seven per cent that John Jacob Astor charged his own business associates in St. Louis for advances. At the upper edge of interest rates there might be charges of from one to two per cent a month, coupled with additional price markups on trade goods if both credit and supplies came from the same factor.

Small trading partnerships might be financed on advances at the price of half their gross take in furs.[10]

Under these pressures, they constantly sought to find new ways to increase the profitability of their ventures. The rendezvous system did not work out particularly well because of the high risks incurred by the mountain men who might carry their proceeds in furs around with them in the Indian country for some months, and because of the basic fault of a once-a-year cash flow cycle that was costly to all participants.[11]

The most important of the new systems tried by the major traders was the building of large, fixed trading posts in the heart of the Indian country. This came about largely through the steady shift from beaver and small furs to Indian tanned buffalo robes as the greatest volume of fur products available in the west. The change was occasioned partly by the cost/price squeeze that continued to plague the beaver trade as it had done for forty years or more. It was hastened by the speed with which the plains tribes commercialized their economy as they became dependent on the traders for guns, ammunition, textiles, tools and increasingly liquor.[12]

Between 1833 and 1841, such major stockaded trading posts as Fort William on the Laramie, "Portugese Houses" on Powder River, Fort Hall in Idaho tapped the plains Indian trade and served as bases of operations for the American trappers.[13]

William Bent built a small timber stockade on the North Bank of the Arkansas around 1824-26, about twenty miles above the mouth of Fountain Creek. Bent developed a close association with the southernmost bands of the Cheyenne Indians.[14] In 1833, he joined forces with his brother Charles Bent and with Ceran St. Vrain to build the massive adobe trading post now called "Bent's Old Fort" on the Arkansas. This post stood six miles downstream from present LaJunta, Colorado about 35 miles from the nearest point in Las Animas County. The firm had extensive mercantile interests in New Mexico and used the mountain branch of the Santa Fe Trail over Raton Pass in its traffic between the two locations.[15]

Drawn by the convenience of Bent's Old Fort, lured southward by the more abundant horse herds in that direction, and pressed from behind by more powerful tribes, the southern Cheyennes relocated in the country along the Arkansas. William Bent strengthened the relationship by marrying two Cheyenne girls. For the next thirty years, this would be Cheyenne country, and the foothills and the mountains a zone of conflict between that tribe and the Utes.[16]

The Bents' combination of Santa Fe trade with Indian trading operations proved profitable enough to attract competition. John Gantt and Jefferson Blackwell built a small post on the north bank of the Arkansas about six miles below Fountain Creek in 1832, but abandoned it in 1835 or earlier.[17]

Perhaps to forestall such upstream competition, Bent, St. Vrain and Company sent Maurice Le Duc to build a trading post beside the Hard-scrabble Trail in the late 1830's.[18]

Mathew Kinkead put up his own ranch and trading post on the Hard-scrabble Trail about 1843.[19]

These two posts served the Ute trade in the mountains while Bent's Fort served the Cheyennes and ultimately the Kiowas and Comanche.

In 1842, an aggregation of mountain men built a fort called "El Pueblo", just a short distance above the mouth of Fountain Creek. Only a few people were here by 1854, when Indians massacred the occupants on Christmas of 1854.[20]

Commancheros built another adobe settlement on the Arkansas about four miles above Bent's Old Fort. Their sale of dairy products to other traders earned this establishment the name of "Milk Fort."[21]

Though the Kinkead establishment and Fort LeDuc were the only trading posts of this era within the Raton Basin, it was well served by the surrounding posts, as well as by itinerant traders operating over trails out of Taos.

That the highly organized trading operations of the Bents did not break down in the 1840's is testimony to their well balanced and carefully managed business system.

From the South Platte country on north to the Powder River country, the classic big-fort Indian trade went through a dramatic change in the 1840's. It soon became apparent that the overhead of the big establishments exceeded the financing capacity of most small partnerships.

Enough commercial and emigrant traffic developed on the main transcontinental trail up the North Platte to support scattered road-ranches. Small traders like the Richards, the Bissonnettes, Guerriers, Guinards and others ran these, relying on their Indian relatives-by-marriage to provide a measure of security from attack. They competed ruthlessly for the Indian trade. Their main competitive edge was straight grain alcohol and their best source for it was Taos.[22]

There, in the 1830's, relocated Kentuckians like Simeon Turley built distilleries using locally available grain grown by the New Mexicans. John Richard and other "Missouri French" traders took this "Taos Lightning" north in pack trains through Raton Pass to serve the Indian trade up on the North Platte.[23]

By the late 1830's, practically all felt for hats was made from cheap furs like racoon instead of the costly beaver fur. In a depressed market, the scattered beaver resources of the Rockies would not support costly trapping operations like those of the 1920's. The buffalo robe trade increased steadily in importance to the traders, but the Indians increasing dependence on liquor reduced their relative productivity in this field.

International conditions further reduced the competitive position of American trading companies. Most major trading partnerships closed down their big forts on the plains in the 1840's. Pierre Chouteau, Jr. and Company, Lancaster P. Lupton and Company both withdrew from the Platte River country in those years.[24]

Solidly entrenched in their own region, the Bents ran their old fort until 1849, and then in 1852 constructed a new one farther down-stream from which they continued to dominate the Indian trade effectively until the beginning of settlement in the late Fifties.[25]

The transition from a traders' frontier to a settlers' frontier was a well-established pattern in the U.S. by this time. Merchants in the New Mexico settlements such as Ceran St. Vrain, Charles Beaubien and others had been raised in Missouri when it was undergoing a similar transition. With an eye to the future, they and their business associates secured land grants under the liberal Mexican laws that gave them a title to vast acreages, some of them within the Raton Basin.

Cornelio Vigil and Ceran St. Vrain obtained their land grant from the Mexican government in 1843. The lands it covered had not been surveyed by the Mexicans, but under the most liberal interpretation it covered around four million acres.

Next in importance was a grant to Charles Beaubien and Guadalupe Miranda that same year. This is better known as the Maxwell Land

31

Grant, since in later years it came under the control of Beaubien's son-in-law, Lucien B. Maxwell.

Another grant, the Nolan Grant covered a large tract near present Pueblo, and extending in part into the Raton Basin.

Together, these land grants covered about half the area of Raton Basin, plus extensive tracts in adjacent Pueblo and Bent Counties and in New Mexico. It was generally assumed that holders of the grants would encourage settlement on the lands by their employees, by lessees and by parties to whom they might sell land.[26]

Before actual settlement on the land grants within the Raton Basin could transpire, the war with Mexico quickly brought the region under U.S. control and ushered in an accellerated pattern of change.

Relations between the U.S. and Mexico had been tense ever since settlers from the U.S. had taken up extensive tracts in east Texas and wrestled control of the area away from Mexico to set up their own independent republic in 1835-36. Mexico was still further outraged when Texas became a part of the United States in 1846.

With the annexation of Texas, the U.S. became a party to the existing boundary dispute between Texas and Mexico. Mexico claimed the Neuces River was the international line, and the U.S. backed Texan claims on land extending to the Rio Grande. President John Tyler forced the issue by sending federal troops into the disputed territory and war broke out.

Action flared on three fronts: Federal reenforcements moved into Texas and across the Rio Grande. A major expeditionary force landed on the Mexican coast at Vera Cruz and drove inland to Mexico City. And the U.S. moved swiftly to seize Mexican ports in California.

General Stephen Watts Kearny moved west with a column of regular Dragoons to capture Mexican settlements in New Mexico and Arizona and to effect the conquest of California in collaboration with navy forces operating in the Pacific. His route took him over the mountain branch of the Santa Fe Trail. Colonel Philip St. George Cooke followed up with a supply column escorted by a volunteer battalion of Mormon recruits from the Missouri River country. New Mexico quickly surrendered to the passing troops. The resettled Missouri traders supported the occupation troops in anticipation of a change of sovereignty.[27]

The war itself lasted but a season. Negotiations on territorial transfers and compensation took longer. While this was going on, Indians at Taos Pueblo revolted against the provisional government. While federal troops and their adherents swiftly put down the uprising, Charles Bent was among the Americans killed by the rebels.[28]

Supply operations brought still more freight traffic over both branches of the Santa Fe Trail, and acquainted still more Americans with the region. Then the Treaty of Guadalupe-Hidalgo turned New Mexico and much other Mexican territory over to the U.S. in 1848. The treaty confirmed Mexican land titles in the New Mexico settlements and thus opened the way for their holders to encourage settlement of these lands.[29]

At the same time, there was the prospect that American control would bring the security from Indian attack that was essential to actual settlement of the land.

NOTES ON CHAPTER III.

1. Isaac J. Cox, "Opening the Santa Fe Trail," *Missouri Historical Review,* Vol. 25, (1930-31), pp. 30-66.

2. Kenyon Riddle, *Records and Maps of the Old Santa Fe Trail,* (Raton, N.Mex.: 1949), Map 3.

3. Margaret Long, "The Santa Fe Trail on the Cimarron..." *Colorado Magazine,* Vol. 14, (1937), pp. 115-118.

4. Carl P. Russell, "Wilderness Rendezvous Period of the American Fur Trade," *Oregon Historical Quarterly,* Vol. 42, (1941), pp. 1-47.

5. Robert A. Murray, "Some Interpretive Notes on the Fur Trade..." *Museum of the Fur Trade Quarterly,* Vol. 3, #3, (Fall, 1967), pp. 1-4.

6. Francois Antoine Larocque, "Journal..." *Sources of Northwest History,* No. 20, (1934), pp. 5ff.

7. Cecil J. Alter, *Jim Bridger,* (Norman: University of Oklahoma Press, 1962), pp. 40-45, citing Utah Fish and Game Commission studies.

8. LeRoy R. Hafen, "Colorado Mountain Men," *Colorado Magazine,* Vol. 30, (1953), pp. 14-28.

9. Janet Lecompte, "Mathew Kinkead," in: *Mountain Men and the Fur Trade,* (Glendale, California: Arthur H. Clark Co., 1965), Vol. 2, pp. 188-199.

   Harvey L. Carter, "Dick Wootten," in: *Mountain Men and the Fur Trade,* (Glendale, California: Arthur H. Clark Co., 1966), Vol. 3, pp. 407-411.

   Janet Lecompte, "Charles Autobees," in: *Mountain Men and the Fur Trade,* (Glendale, California: Arthur H. Clark Co., 1966), Vol. 4, pp. 21-37.

10. Robert A. Murray, "Fur Trade of the Fort Laramie Region," in *Fort Laramie, Visions of a Grand Old Post,* (Fort Collins, Colorado: Old Army Press, 1974), pp. 10-13.

11. *ibid.,* p. 11-12.

12. *ibid.,* p. 12.

13. LeRoy R. Hafen and Francis M. Young, *Fort Laramie and the Pageant of the West,* (Glendale, California: Arthur H. Clark Co., 1940), pp. 1-110.

Edgely W. Todd, "Antonio Montero," in: *Mountain Men and the Fur Trade*, (Glendale, Arthur H. Clark Co., 196), Vol. 6, pp. 101-103.

14. Samuel P. Arnold, "William W. Bent," in: *Mountain Men and the Fur Trade*, (Glendale: Arthur H. Clark Co., 1968), Vol. 6, pp. 61-84.

15. David Lavender, *Bent's Old Fort*, (N.Y.: Doubleday, 19), pp.

16. Donald J. Berthrong, *The Southern Cheyennes*, (Norman: Univeristy of Oklahoma Press, 1968), pp.

17. Lavender, *op. cit.*, pp. 380-381.

18. Janet Lecompte, "Maurice LeDuc," in: *Mountain Men and the Fur Trade*, (Glendale: Arthur H. Clark Co., 1968), Vol. 6, pp. 227-240.

19. Janet Lecompte, "Mathew Kinkead," in: *Mountain Men and the Fur Trade*, (Glendale, California: Arthur H. Clark Co., 1965), Vol. 2, pp. 188-199.

20. Raymond M. Beckner, *Along Colorado Trails*, (Pueblo, Colorado: O'Brien Stationery, 1975), pp. 17-18.

21. Lavender, *op. cit.*, pp. 382-385.

22. LeRoy R. Hafen, editorial introduction in: *Mountain Men and the Fur Trade*, (Glendale, California: Arthur H. Clark Co., 1965), Vol. 1, pp. 157-176.

23. Janet Lecompte, "Simeon Turley," in: *Mountain Men and the Fur Trade*, (Glendale, California: Arthur H. Clark Co., 1969), Vol. 7, pp. 302-303.

24. Hafen & Young, *op. cit.*, pp. 135-142.

25. Lavender, *op. cit.*, pp. 317 ff.

26. Richard W. Bradfute, "The Las Animas Land Grant, 1843-1900," *Colorado Magazine*, Vol. 47, #1, (Winter, 1970), pp. 26-43.

27. Lavender, *op. cit.*, pp. 284-297.

    also: Leo E. Oliva, *Soldiers on the Santa Fe Trail*, (Norman: University of Oklahoma Press, 19), pp. 21 ff.

28. Lavender, *op. cit.*, pp. 275-289.

29. John E. Oster, "Diplomatic and Treaty Relations Between the United States and Mexico," *Hispanic American Historical Review*, Vol. 7, (1927), pp. 2-24.

Chapter IV. EARLY SETTLEMENT YEARS

While the ratification of the Treaty of Guadalupe-Hidalgo in 1848
cleared the way for Anglo-American settlers to move into the country
south of the Arkansas, there was no immediate rush to the Raton Basin.
The main frontier of settlement lay almost five-hundred miles to the
east in Missouri. It also took a while for New Mexican settlers to
start to move into the region in any numbers. Their hesitancy came in
part from the hazard of Indian attack, and the small number of existing
nuclei for settlement. Only at Fort Pueblo near Fountain Creek, around
the LeDuc and Kinkead trading posts on Hardscrabble, and downstream on
the Arkansas at Milk Fort and Bent's Fort were there existing settlements in or near the Raton Basin.[1]

Though the treaty confirmed Mexican land titles, some uncertainties
remained about the way in which the U.S. Courts might handle the interpretation of these titles, in particular the large land grants.

So, settlement proceeded slowly. Charles Autobees and a few other
old mountaineers established Autobees Plaza at the mouth of the Huerfano
River in 1853.[2]

John Wesley Prowers, an employee of the Bents, brought out 600 head
of cattle from Missouri in 1861. Encouraged by the potential market in
the new gold-camps of northern Colorado, he added a hundred stock-cows
to his herds in 1862. In these early years Prowers ranged his cattle
from the Purgatory east to the Kansas line, south of the Arkansas. They
were the first resident "range cattle" herds that spilled over into the
Raton Basin.[3]

John C. Dawson brought a herd of cattle up from Texas to sell in
the Colorado mining camps in 1859, pioneering one of the trails used by
later cattlemen. Dawson's trail entered the territory along the north

side of the Arkansas River and followed that stream to Fountain Creek, where it turned north, roughly paralleling present Interstate 25 to the Denver area.[4]

By 1864, other cattlemen brought as many as a hundred-thousand stock cattle to Colorado, but the importance of the gold-camp market led most of them to put their cattle on ranges close to Denver and the northern Colorado mining towns. Charles Goodnight pioneered a new route for Texas cattle in 1864 when his herds came up the Pecos to its headwaters and then entered Colorado by either Trinchera Pass or Raton Pass according to range conditions on a given drive.[5]

The most numerous settlers in the Raton Basin during the early 1860's, however, came from New Mexico. Colonel J.M. Francisco, a Virginian merchant, set up Francisco Fort or Francisco Plaza in 1862, attracting employees and settlers from New Mexico. This settlement later became the nucleus for the town of LaVeta.[6]

Detailed land-title research would be required to sort out the precise dates of all the early settlements. It is known that the Madrid family formed Madrid Plaza, on the Purgatory above present Trinidad around 1864.[7] State Senator J.M. Madrid, of that family, interviewed in the early 1930's, recollected a total of nineteen early settlements on the Purgatory above Trinidad. Of these a dozen would appear to have been the "plaza" variety of group-family or extended family settlements.[8]

The Barela family came from New Mexico to found their settlement on San Francisco Creek in 1866.[9] Torres Plaza and Vigil Plaza were founded by other New Mexican families in about the same period.[10]

Some of the plazas, as well as some of the early ranches established by anglo settlers occupied lands obtained at nominal cost from

40

The traditional Spanish adobe and the rough canvas of the settler
meet at the Old Plaza, La Veta, Colorado. *Colorado Historical Society.*

holders of the major land grants.[11] This posed a peril until the land grant titles were clarified.

In 1854, Congress set up the office of Surveyor General for New Mexico and charged it with detailing the terms and the legal standing of the Mexican land grants of the former New Mexico province, and making recommendations to Congress relative the confirmation of the titles.[12] The first Surveyor General of New Mexico, William Pelham, recommended simply that the grants be confirmed.[13]

For three years after receiving this recommendation, the Senate Committee on Private Land Claims debated the legal status of the claims. The controversy arose out of the fact that some of the grants had been made subsequent to a Mexican law of 1828 that had placed a statutory limit on such grants that might be obtained by one individual. Several of the grants of course were in the names of partnerships or other associations.[14]

After extensive discussion, Congress passed a law in 1860 that specifically dealt with each of the grants. The Beaubien-Miranda Grant (now controlled by Lucien Maxwell) was confirmed in its full amount of over two million acres. So were some of the other grants in New Mexico.

But the most important grant to the Raton Basin, the Vigil and St. Vrain Grant was specifically limited to 97,000 acres of land. From this amount, certain lands already sold had to be deducted. Squatters living on the lands of the grant were to be relocated outside its limits on the public lands.[15]

The severe limitation by Congress upon the Vigil and St. Vrain Grant set in motion a complex pattern of litigation that extended until 1900. For St. Vrain and his associates had already sold deeds to parcels

42

of land totaling much more than 97,000 acres of land to ranchers, developers and other settlers! Some of these deeds had reverted to the original grant holders through death or default of purchasers before their contracts were fulfilled. Other tracts had been passed on to still other purchasers. Lawyers and surveyors profited substantially from the controversies that came up from time to time.[16]

The Nolan Grant encountered still more problems arising out of the circumstances of its transfer in the years before U.S. jurisdiction, and the courts reduced its acreage sharply in 1870.[17]

Important as it was to the nation in general, the Civil War had little impact on southern Colorado. The nearest action took place well inside New Mexico at Glorieta Pass. Units of the Colorado Volunteers were involved in the New Mexico campaign, though, and this military activity increased the demand for beef and grain in the region.[18]

Local folklore holds that for a time a band of Confederate sympathizers hid out in a place called "Mace's Hole," near present Buelah, hoping to join Confederate troops that they expected to come up out of New Mexico. These irregulars dispersed when the Colorado Volunteers turned back the Confederates decisively at Glorieta Pass.[19]

With the troops away, Indian depredations increased for a time. Utes swept down through the Raton Basin to attack scattered settlements along the Arkansas in 1863.[20] The Cheyennes committed a number of depredations on the plains of northeastern Colorado. Retalitory campaigns by the Colorado Volunteers, such as the Sand Creek affair with the Cheyennes, were well removed from the Raton Basin.[21]

So, for the most part, the new settlements of the mid-Sixties developed as their founders wanted them to. For the New Mexican settlers,

they took the form of traditional New Mexico villages. These plazas
tended to be economically self-sufficient units. Each community con-
sisted of a group of extended families.

Each plaza was dominated by the senior male head of an important
family, called the patron.

In some cases he was a principal Landowner. In others he served as
an intermediary between the peons and the landowner or an organization
controlling the land grant involved. He spent a great deal of time
functioning as a business counselor for his people. He was the sole
source of credit. He owned the mercantile establishment at the plaza.
Yet, despite the dominance of one man, the pattern of mutual responsibilities for services tended to balance what was given for what was
received, so long as the community retained a high degree of self-
sufficiency. When this self-sufficiency was imperiled by an increasingly commercial economy in the surrounding region, the internal relationships of the plaza came under stress, and ultimately broke down.[22]

Sheep ranchers of the early settlement period were usually New
Mexicans, integrated into the system by familial links with the communities near which their stock ranged.[23]

But the cattlemen were another matter entirely. They were, for the
most part Texas frontiersmen who came from a society less rigidly organized than that of the New Mexican settlers. They owed their next level
of fealty to the government, and this was for many a very loose tie in
view of the outcome of the recent Civil War. From 1864 to the early
1870's there was unrestricted competition between cattlemen for range,
and after that date only the beginnings of cattlemen's organizations for
their mutual advantage.

Army operations between 1864 and 1870 cleared the plains of eastern Colorado of hostile Indians. Proximity to substantial markets, access to the advancing railhead towns on the Kansas Pacific Railroad, along with the generally good wintering conditions in southern Colorado all helped stimulate the cattle industry in the Raton Basin.

Throughout the early Seventies, cattlemen consolidated their hold on much of the grazing land within and immediately east of the Raton Basin. Even in the first few years of the decade, they began on a local basis to organize stockmen's associations to deal with access to water, regulation of rustling, competition with the sheep men, and to secure more effective communication with government agencies.[24]

Some communities grew up around trading posts that were not strictly organized along traditional New Mexico lines. Often they tended to serve both the anglo and latin communities. Francisco Plaza developed in this direction, and so did the community that grew up around the trading post of Fred Walsen and grew ultimately into the town of Walsenburg.[25]

There were other early and heterogenous settlements. When, in 1866, the Colorado Legislature trimmed off most of original Huerfano county to form parts of Las Animas County, Fremont County and Bent County, the Huerfano County Seat was moved from its original location at Autobees Plaza to Badito, a village that had grown up around an important stock-crossing.[26] Likewise, the county seat for newly-created Las Animas County was placed at Trinidad, Colorado, the commercial focal point of the upper Purgatory River plazas, and now the entrance to Raton Pass.[27]

Yet another kind of settlement had some influence on the development of the Raton Basin. These were the "colonies" or organized groups of emigrants. Two such groups were directly involved in the early settlement of the area.

The major group was the "German Colony," organized among German immigrants residing in the midwest. This group formed a company called "the National Land Company" organized as a corporation.

They elected officers and agreed upon cooperative responsibilities in a fashion somewhat similar to the Union Colony that had settled the Greeley, Colorado area a few years earlier.

Carl Wulsten, Rudolph Jeske and Herman Henlein made a reconaissance on behalf of the group in 1869 and selected a potential settlement site in the Wet Mountain Valley. Politically agressive in the fashion of midwestern Lutheran Germans of the period, the group secured the support of the Federal government and Vice President Schuyler Colfax in arranging transportation and a military escort from the end of track on the Kansas Pacific Railroad. About 90 families totaling over 350 persons made the trip in 1870.

They came out to their new high-valley home and selected homesites while their leaders tried to get governmental support for a special land-grant bill. Failing this, they located individual holdings under the Homestead Act of 1862, and secured townsites such as Colfax, Dora, and Ula under other land laws.

Their independent nature, the dispersed pattern of settlement that homesteading compelled, and dissension within the leadership all worked against them. Most of the colonists had little experience in farming. Their organized efforts collapsed in 1872, and by 1874 even the Colfax

Immigrants trekked across the hostile plains in order to take up homesteads in the Raton Basin. *Union Pacific Railroad Archives.*

post office had closed.

Some of the colonists stayed in the Wet Mountain Valley as farmers and ranchers. Others moved to urban centers such as Denver. Wulsten established himself as a mining promoter and achieved some prominence in the mining towns discussed in a later chapter of this paper.[28]

About eight families of French ancestry, among them those with surnames of Garnier, Mercier and Albert settled along the western edge of West Mountain Valley in this same period. A few Mormon families from Salt Lake settled on Taylor Creek. Neither the French nor the Mormons were organized in the same manner as the German group.[29]

Another organized group of settlers who came to the Raton Basin in 1870 were the Georgians, under the leadership of old Green Russell of Colorado Gold Rush fame. They scattered out on ranches in the Huerfano drainage where they were joined by other southern emigrants through the early 1870's.[30]

So, by the early 1870's the Raton Basin was widely but thinly settled by a ranching and subsistence farming population. Their livestock could be driven to distant markets, but other produce was largely for home consumption. Any expansion of their economy awaited the coming of more efficient transportation, as did any effective development of mineral resources.

NOTES ON CHAPTER IV.

1. See foregoing chapter.

2. Janet LeCompte, "Charles Autobees," in: *Mountain Men and the Fur Trade*, (Glendale, California: Arthur H. Clark Co., 1966), Vol. 4, p. 37.

3. Ora B. Peake, *The Colorado Range Cattle Industry*, (Glendale, California: Arthur H. Clark Co., 1937), contains the best overall synthesis of the business from its inception up to the mid 1930's. Prowers career is summarized in the La Junta Tribune, Dec. 15, 1933.

4. Peake, *op. cit.*, pp. 71.

5. J. Evetts Haley, *Charles Goodnight*, (Boston, Houghton-Mifflin, 1936), pp. 130-142.

6. Raymond M. Beckner, *Old Forts of Southern Colorado*, (Pueblo, Colorado: O'Brien Printing and Stationery Co., 1975), pp. 54-55.

7. A. K. Richeson, "Senator J. M. Madrid, Trinidad, Colorado," unpublished document #359/6, CWA files for Las Animas County, in the Colorado Historical Socity, Denver.

8. *ibid.*

9. Wiliam B. Taylor and Elliott West, "Patron Leadership at the Crossroads: Southern Colorado in the Late 19th Century," *Pacific Historical Review*, Vol. 42, #3, (August, 1973), pp. 335-357.

10. Richeson, *op. cit.*

11. Richeson, *op. cit.*, Beckner, *op. cit.*, p. 55.

12. Richard W. Bradfute, "The Las Animas Land Grant, 1843-1900," *Colorado Magazine*, Vol. 47, #1 (Winter, 1970), pp. 26-43.

    also: *House Report 195*, 36th Congress, 1st Session, (1860), and *Senate Report 228*, 36th Congress, 1st Session (1860), pp. 1-3.

13. Morris Taylor, "Captain William Craig and the Vigil and St. Vrain Land Grant, 1855-1870," *Colorado Magazine*, Vol. 45, (Fall, 1968), p. 319.

14. *House Report 195 and Senate Report 228*, *op. cit.*, contain the main substance of the controversy.

15. "An Act to Confirm Certain Private Land Claims in the Territory of New Mexico," *U.S. Statutes at Large*, Vol. 12, (1859-63), p. 71 ff.

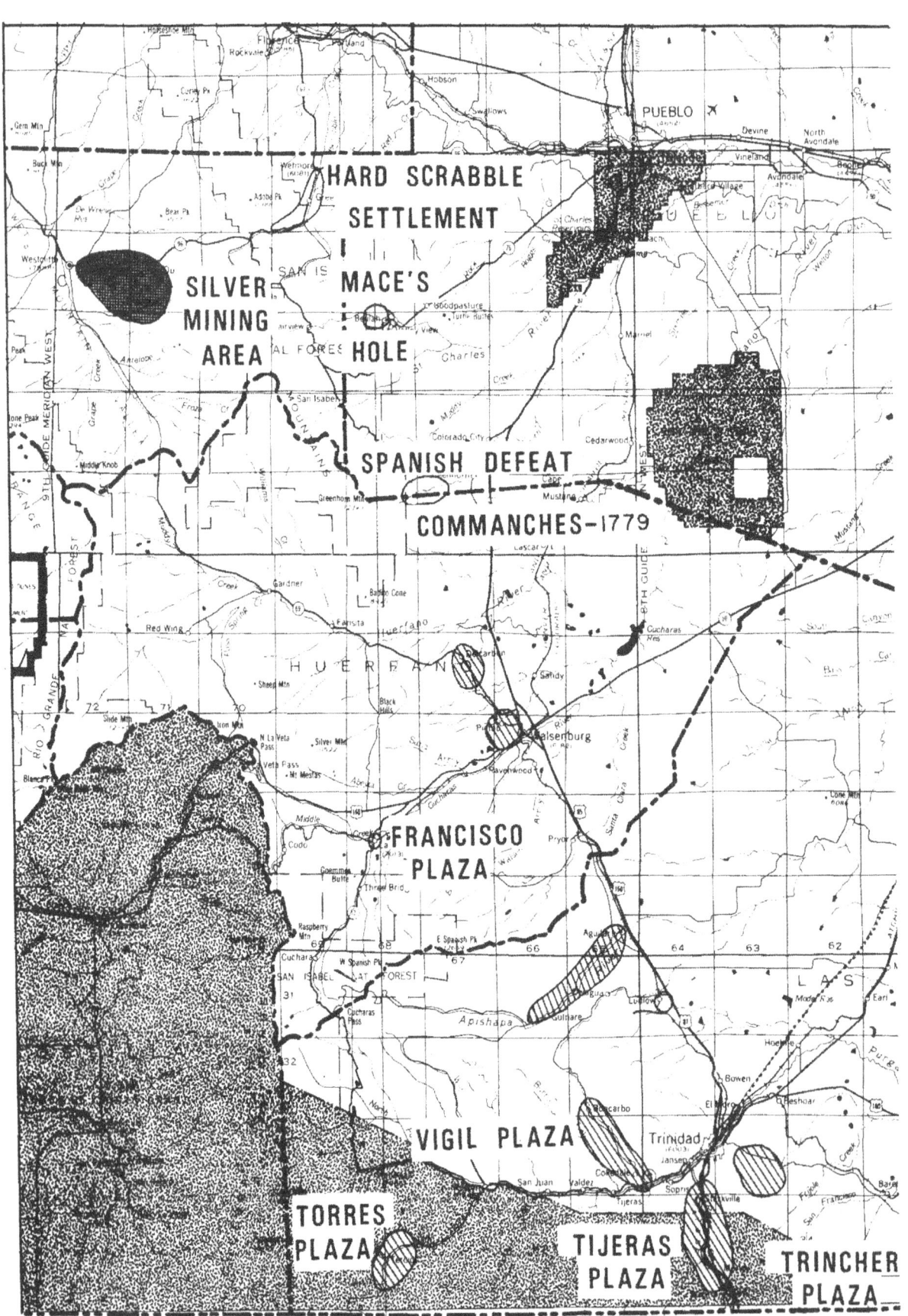

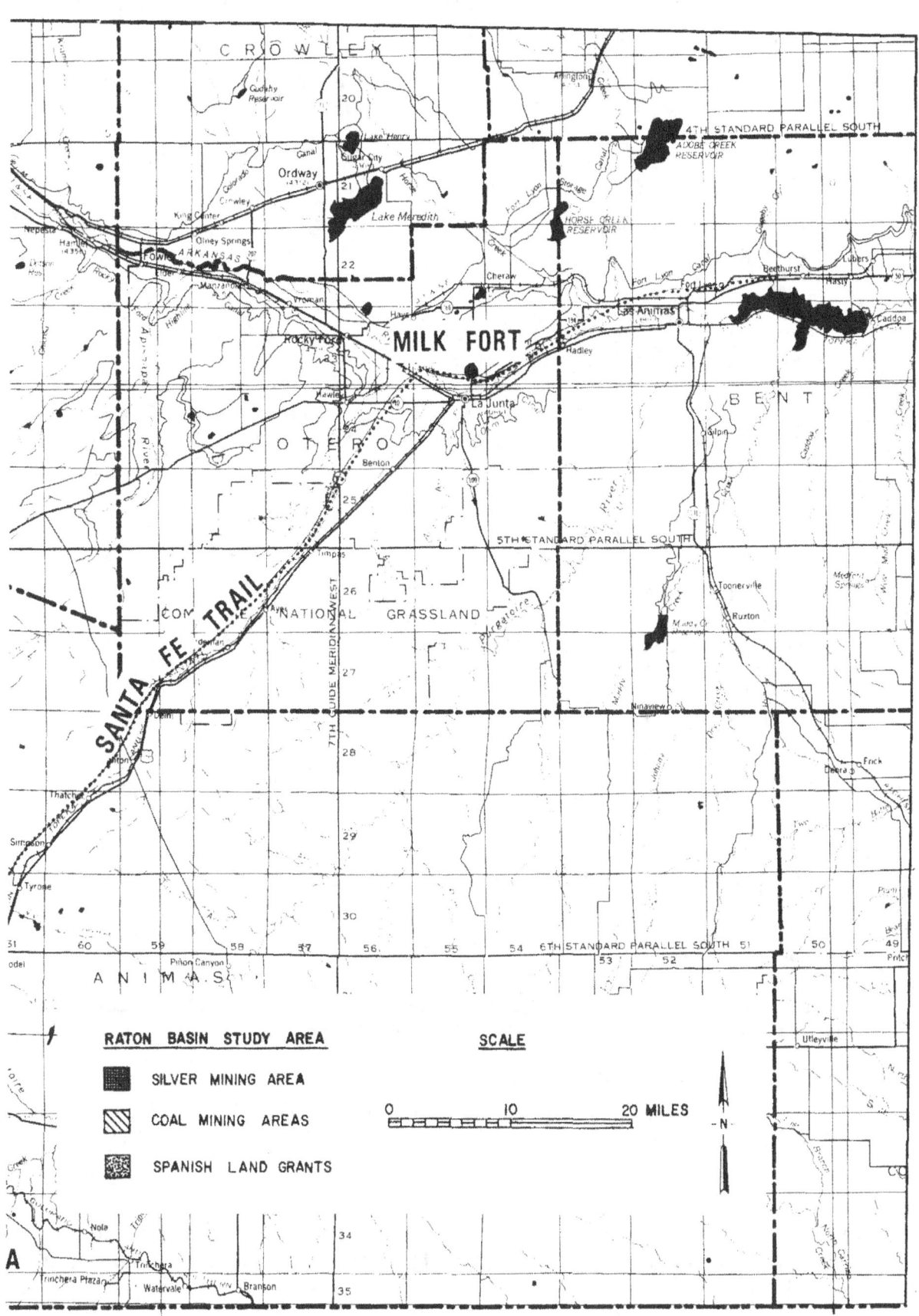

CROWLEY

Gooseby
Reservoir

20

Lake Henry
Sugar City

Ordway

21   Lake Meredith

Canal

King Center
Crowley
Nepesta   Olney Springs
Hamilton   Fowler
ARKANSAS   22
Manzanola   Cheraw

Rocky Ford   **MILK FORT**

La Junta

OTERO   Benton

25

Timpas

COMANCHE NATIONAL GRASSLAND

26

27

28

Thatcher

29

Simpson

Tyrone

30

60   59   58   57   56   55   54   6TH STANDARD PARALLEL SOUTH 51   50   49

Piñon Canyon

ANIMAS

4TH STANDARD PARALLEL SOUTH
ADOBE CREEK
RESERVOIR

Fort Lyon   Canal
HORSE CREEK
RESERVOIR

Fort Lyon   Canal
Beethurst   Lubers
Hasty

Las Animas   Caddoa

BENT

Gilpin

5TH STANDARD PARALLEL SOUTH

Medicine
Springs
Toonerville
Ruxton

Ninaview

Frick

Delora

SANTA FE TRAIL

Utleyville

RATON BASIN STUDY AREA   SCALE

SILVER MINING AREA

COAL MINING AREAS   0   10   20 MILES

SPANISH LAND GRANTS   N

Nola

34

Trinchera

Trinchera Plaza   Watervale   Branson   35

A

51

16. Bradfute, *op. cit.,* pp. 29-41.

17. LeRoy R. Hafen, "Mexican Land Grants in Colorado," *Colorado Magazine,* Vol. 4, (1927), pp. 81-93.

18. Blance V. Adams, "The Second Colorado Cavalry in the Civil War," *Colorado Magazine,* Vol. 8, (1931), pp. 95-106.

19. Raymond M. Beckner, *Along Colorado Trails,* (Pueblo, Colorado: O'Brien Printing and Stationery Co. 1975), pp. 138-142.

20. James Warren Covington, "Federal Relations with the Colorado Utes, 1861-1865," *Colorado Magazine,* Vol. 28, (1951), pp. 257-266.

21. Stan Hoig, *The Sand Creek Massacre,* (Norman: Oklahoma University Press, 1963), describes in fair detail the movements of the troops in pursuit of the Cheyennes throughout the campaign.

22. William B. Taylor and Elliott West, "Patron Leadership at the Crossroads: Southern Colorado in the Late 19th Century, *Pacific Historical Review,* Vol. 42, #3, (August, 1973), pp. 335-357, pp. 389-408.

23. *ibid.,* pp. 335-357.

24. T. R. Feherenbach, *Comanches....,* *op. cit.,* pp. 293-304, details the adaptation of the Anglo-American Texans to frontier life and the development of their relationships with the Latin and Indian cultures they contacted.

    Ora B. Peake, *The Colorado Range Cattle Industry,* (Glendale: Arthur H. Clark Co., 1937), devotes over half its more than 300 pages to adaptive and organizational efforts of the cattlemen of the southern Colorado area.

25. letter, "B" to the editor of the *Colorado Chieftain,* dated May 8, 1874, and printed in the *Chieftain* for May 13, 1874, under the headline "Huerfano County," on p. 1.

26. *ibid.*

27. A. W. McHendrie, "Trinidad and Its Environs," *Colorado Magazine,* Vol. 6, #5, (September 1929), pp. 159-170.

28. Raymond Gardner Colwell, "The Wet Mountain Valley...," unpublished manuscript in the files of Colorado Historical Society, pp. 10-16.

29. *ibid.,* pp. 9-10.

30. Benton Canon, "The History of the Georgia Colony," Document 363/1, pp. 139-146 in the CWA interview MSS for Huerfano County, Colorado Historical Society.

Chapter V.

DIVERSIFICATION OF ECONOMIC DEVELOPMENT

The mid-1870's brought rapid and diversified change to this stock-growers' and subsistence-farmers' country. Many different events occurred swiftly.

Railroads converged on the Raton Basin, bringing first a construction boom and then more rapid access to markets and supply sources. The railroads created the initial demand for serious commercial mining of coal resources in the area. The railroads thus both faciliated and benefited from the boom.

Mining activities brought in new technical specialists as well as new ethnic groups of laborers.

The overall changes drastically uprooted the entrenched economic and political structures of the region. A fully commercialized economy was achieved by the end of the century. In the process, towns came and went, fortunes rose and fell with regularity.

Heavy freight in the early 1870's moved as it had always moved. Slowly, and expensively the freight wagons drawn by oxen or by mules, pushed over the same trails the trappers had inherited from the Indians of the region, like the Hardscrabble Trail and the route over Raton Pass.

The only significant improvement to transportation for the Raton Basin before the mid-Seventies was the construction of a toll-road over Raton Pass by Richens L. "Uncle Dick" Wootton, who secured a strip of land over the pass from the holders of the Maxwell Land Grant.

He then petitioned the Territorial Legislature for a toll-road charter, which that body granted in 1865. Wootton made improvements on the grade through extensive rock cut and fill work, and he built a number of bridges. His road proved to be a popular shortcut to the New

Mexico settlements, and he derived a substantial income from the tolls[1].

But in general, the economy of the area remained a stockman's economy, for livestock was the only product that could carry itself to market.

Communications were limited to mail service offered by the U.S. government, with the mail actually transported by contract carriers and mostly by the stage lines.

The Raton Basin was well off the major transcontinental lines of communication, so mail and passenger service developed more slowly than it did for points such as Fort Collins, Colorado in the northernmost part of the territory.

In 1869, there was only a tri-weekly service between Pueblo and Santa Fe. Allowing for time en route and a chance to reply, many people found that the simplest exchange of letters between Pueblo and Trinidad took at least ten days.[2]

People in this section of Colorado were treated to the hope of rail service with the Denver and Rio Grande Railway Company was incorporated in both Colorado and New Mexico in the fall of 1870. The company began to push its narrow-gauge line southward from Denver in 1871, reaching Colorado Springs, Colorado that same year.

In 1872, the line reached Pueblo, Colorado and a branch was built to Florence, Colorado. In effect, this gave two railheads that could be reached from portions of Raton Basin. Then, with the Denver and Rio Grande absorbed in construction activity elsewhere and with capital hard to obtain, the rails stopped for a time at those two towns.

Resumption of construction activity that brought the railroad into the Raton Basin was closely linked to the coal resources there. William Jackson Palmer and other railroad investors speculatively purchased

One of the most important events in the history of the Raton Basin
was the coming of the railroads. Seen here is a Denver and Rio
Grande Railroad train at La Veta Pass. *Colorado Historical Society.*

large blocks of coal land that could be developed with the coming of a railroad.

Competition, or the threat of it, also forced the D. & R.G.'s hand. The Atchison, Topeka and Santa Fe railroad built a standard gauge line into Pueblo, Colorado in 1876. The D. & R.G. then commenced laying track southward, and in April of 1876 reached El Moro, Colorado, five miles from Trinidad, Colorado. This caused considerable local dissatisfaction, since El Moro was a company town, created by the railroad, and Trinidad merchants did not like such competition.

The D. & R.G. was faced with the approach of the Santa Fe on several fronts, so it concentrated on building from Cucharas, Colorado to LaVeta, Colorado and on over LaVeta Pass into the San Luis Valley. With the railroad reaching most key points in the Raton Basin, economic development proceeded at a sharply accellerated pace.

Early in 1878, the Santa Fe suddenly seized the best construction route over Raton Pass and built a line southwest of La Junta, Colorado into New Mexico. Now the region had an abundance of rail service.[3] Within two years the economy began to change, and with it came social changes that were irreversible. The most important of these centered around coal mining.

As indicated in the description of the natural setting, the sedimentary formations immediately in front of the mountains in this area contain extensive coal layers. When igneous intrusions came in contact with the coal, they burned off gasses and carbon, destroying the deposit. Where they came just close enough to create a high heat level, the lignite and sub-bituminous coals were changed to a high-density bituminous coal, suitable for coking.[4]

Accessible deposits of coking coal occur in few places in the Rockies. The cost of rail transport for coke at first limited the development of large scale smelting operations in the region. Coal outcrops in the Raton Basin were observed by early settlers and explorers. Dr. F.M. Endlich of the F.V. Hayden U.S. Geological Surveys examined the deposits of this area in 1875 and reported upon them at about the same time that William J. Palmer and other speculators were starting to buy up coal lands.[5]

With railroads at hand, only development time was needed to open up the coal deposits. This work began in 1876. Commercial mining began near Walsenburg, Colorado at the Walsen Mine in 1881. Mines near Trinidad in the late 1870's were developed to feed the coke ovens constructed at El Moro, Colorado. By the early 1880's these were reported to be the largest coke manufacturing facilities west of Pittsburg.[6]

The largest mines were owned by the Colorado Coal and Iron Company, which merged with the Colorado Fuel Company in 1892 to form the Colorado Fuel and Iron Company. This organization built a complex of smelters and steel mills near Pueblo, Colorado. At the outset it used coal from the Canon City, Colorado mines, but plant capacity expanded rapidly, so that soon the smelters used much of the production from the Trinidad and Walsenburg mines as well.[7]

Other, smaller producers supplied important quantities of coal to the markets of the region. One of these was the Wootton Fuel and Timber Company[8] and another the Victor Fuel Company. By the year 1900, mines in the Trinidad, Colorado area employed over 8,000 men and the smaller operations at Walsenburg, Colorado around 300.[9]

C.F. and I. looked far afield for sources of iron ore sufficiently rich to pay the cost of shipment to Pueblo. Prospecting for ore in Wyoming, the company found sufficient deposits of hematite in the Hartville Hills, and began shipping ore from their Sunrise Mine there in 1898.[10]

With the high grade iron ore available, smelting operations expanded rapidly, and with them of course coal production rose quickly to over a million tons per year.[11]

The Trinidad area mines spread over a wider area than those at Walsenburg. With broader access to the coal seams, they developed into the major producers of the region. A number of Company towns served the mines. Major ones were:

> Starkville: located south of Trinidad, this and its mines were developed by the Santa Fe railroad, but sold to C.F. & I. in 1896.
>
> Engleville, which supplied the coke ovens at El Moro for C.F. and I.
>
> Cokedale, and its Mount Carmel Mine, which belonged to the American Smelting and Refining Company.
>
> Hastings, Delagua, Bowen and Gray Creek, all belonging to the Victor American Fuel Company.
>
> The Jewell Mine, two miles from Aguilar and the Dick mine in Riley Canyon were operated by Dick Brothers.

As the new century opened, C.F. and I. had plans under way to open a large number of additional mines.[12]

Steady expansion of the population of the mining towns created a ready local market for agricultural produce. At the same time, the railroads brought the ranchers and farmers into better contact with more distant markets. So, the same era that saw an expansion of business activity in the mining towns brought growth and change in the country-side as well.

The open range cattle business of the mid-1870's operated upon simple lines. Until competition developed, not many of the cattlemen invested in a significant amount of land. They simply pushed their cattle out on public domain lands, and rounded them up seasonally, just as the early cattlemen from Texas had done. Sometimes they made a homestead filing on a site for headquarters, horse corrals and a small tract of hay ground. The headquarters might consist of a log or adobe house, with possibly a bunkhouse for half a dozen or less year around employees. Often the cattlemen did not even bother to acquire ownership of such a site in the early years.

Everything was built as cheaply as possible. Likewise, the lowest cost labor served the industry. In this period a cowboy could expect to earn thirty dollars a month and his food and shelter.[13]

With a small outlay for capital and labor, the cattlemen put virtually all their money into cattle as fast as they could bring them into the region. On paper the profits looked good. By the late 1870's Dr. Hiram Latham's book *Trans-Missouri Stock Raising*, received widespread circulation. Latham described the apparent profits of open range grazing in southern Wyoming and in northern Colorado. Soon another book, *Cattle Raising on the Plains of North America* by Walter, Baron von Richtofen, described the specific situation in northeastern Colorado. A third book, *The Beef Bonanza, or How to Get Rich on the Plains*, by Brevet Brigadier General James S. Brisbin, reached an even greater audience.[14]

Large ranchers began to seek outside capital with which to buy more cattle. Aided by the publicity generated by the three books cited, and by a wealth of newspaper coverage of the industry, they found it. Much of it came from eastern investors, some came from financial sources in France and Germany, and a very large amount came from British investors.

Most major regional accounts of the rise and decline of the old open range cattle industry deal with the general over expansion of the industry, the effects of careless management practices, and the impact of settlement that cut off water sources and winter grazing lands, and with the results of several regional droughts, hard winters and the like.[15] Despite the connections and the parallels of some of these conditions that apply to wide areas, there are significant local differences that apply in the Raton Basin.

First, it is evident that many of the early settlers gained control of the choice sites that could be used as a base for ranching operations. The emigrants from New Mexico had considerable experience at both cattle and sheep raising in an arid region. Where they could, they took up lands that controlled access to water.[16]

Some of them combined their own solid stock raising traditions with considerable managerial talent and quick adaptation to the Anglo economic system. By the mid-Seventies, a number of these Spanish speaking ranchers were well established and could hold their own on the range. The family of Casimiro Barela is one example. They quickly extended their activities from ranching into a continuing involvement in the politics of Las Animas County and of the State.[17]

Fencing of water sources and of sizeable blocks of public domain lands proceeded faster here than in the northern plains. In general, the impression is left that by 1882, the range was cut up into fairly well-defined ranches, in contrast to the situation in Wyoming, for example, where the open range lasted well into the 'Nineties.[18]

This process was aided by the existence of the Mexican land grants. The Prairie Cattle Company leased grazing rights from owners of the Maxwell Land Grant in the southern part of the Raton Basin and used this as the core for considerable holdings on surrounding public lands. On the grant itself there was no worry about settlers coming in to homestead water sources. The company made Trinidad, Colorado its headquarters, with the regional manager, Murdo McKenzie residing there.[19]

The Nolan Land Grant gave an early start to the San Carlos Ranch. Within the Vigil and St. Vrain claims there were the Hermosilla and the Butler ranches.[20]

Barbed wire fencing came on the market in 1875-76, and cheap rail transportation brought it into the Raton Basin before it reached places like Wyoming or Montana in quantity. Companies operating on the big land grants enclosed their holdings first, but major ranchers also enclosed large tracts of public domain lands with wire, and set off many small local conflicts with others who wished to graze the public lands. By 1882, there were complaints of illegal fencing from headsteaders who wished to locate along the streams, from travelers forced out of their way by locked gates, and by migrant stockmen. Special Agent H.W. Jones of the General Land Office staff in Pueblo, Colorado complained to the Secretary of the Interior in that year, and cited a number of examples. But investigation moved slowly over the next few years.[21]

The cattle industry was a major portion of the Raton Basin's
economy as is seen in this branding operation. *Photo courtesy
Don Dutro, Ft. Benton, Montana.*

The problem of fencing on the public domain lands received a great deal of publicity nationally by the mid 1880's. Responding to public pressure, expressed through Congress, the Interior Department forced many ranches to remove illegal fences that enclosed public lands. Within the Raton Basin, Hall and Barela took down their fences around 38,000 acres of land. The Prairie Cattle Company removed fences from 36,000 acres of public domain lands in this period.[22]

Ranchers could of course enclose their private lands, and within the Raton Basin much of the land along streams and around springs passed into private hands by the early 1880's. With effective control of the intervening range, cattlemen in this area invested in highgrade animals at an earlier time than is characteristic of either the northern plains or the desert ranges of the southwest.

Better control of herds, plus the milder winters of the foothills and plains within the Raton Basin made wintering of cattle in the region less risky than it was in the northern Colorado and Wyoming range lands. Colorado had a hard winter in 1881-82 that extended into the area with only modest impact. The Raton Basin missed entirely the disastrous winter of 1886-1887 that swept the plains from the Platte Valley clear into Canada.[23]

In those northern regions, the hard winter offered a good excuse to clear the books of imaginary "book count" cattle that padded them during the peak of the foreign investment boom. It also revealed the fallacy of untended wintering of cattle without supplemental feed on the open range, for real losses ranged from ten to fifty per cent in that region.[24] But here in the Raton Basin the main impact of the in-dustry-wide reaction to the northern hard winter came in the form of revised management practices and a closer look by investors that produced a shortage of working capital.

Despite the losses elsewhere, there were still plenty of cattle ready for market from the long overstocked ranges. Cattle prices remained low through that decade, while other economic activities in the Raton Basin forged ahead.[25]

Sheep ranching developed parallel to cattle ranching except that it did not go through a disastrous boom-and-bust phase in the same way that cattle raising did. The first New Mexican emigrants to the Raton Basin brought a strong and systematic sheep raising tradition with them.

Earlier control of grazing lands helped both latin and anglo ranching families make an effective transition to mixed sheep and cattle operations sooner than occurred elsewhere in the State. This was accomplished without the violence that accompanied the process in some other regions of the West, such as southwestern Wyoming or north central Arizona.[26]

Raton Basin ranchers did support the general state wide move for State-supported irrigation development in 1880's and early 1890's, and two public irrigation storage projects started in those years.

Governor Alva Adams brought together many regional requests for such projects into a state-wide water development plan, and presented it to the Colorado General Assembly. As passed by that body in 1891, the plan authorized a state-financed project in Custer County and   in Las Animas County.

The projects were to be financed by withdrawals from the account used for deposit of the five per cent federal rebate on public domain land sales.[27]

The Custer County Reservoir was an off-stream project, drawing its water from Hardscrabble Creek. Built at a cost of $9,250, the reservoir held just over four and a quarter million cubic feet of water, and covered 11.74 acres. [28]

The Las Animas County project was called the Apishapa Reservoir, but was located in Metote Canyon and drew its water supply from Trujillo Creek about two miles away. This impoundment was somewhat larger, designed for 20,000,000 cubic feet of storage. [29]

Both of the projects were completed in 1892. The legislators felt the benefit from such projects was local in its effect, so the Assembly repeatedly rejected proposals for state funding of maintenance of the projects. In 1899 they were turned over to the counties. The reservoirs supplied for   years a modest reserve of irrigation water for down-stream hay ground for the ranchers. [30]

In the period 1875 to 1900, then ranching consolidated its operations and remained an important part of the Raton Basin economy. But in the overall economic and political picture it quickly took a place well behind the developing mining towns, and it is within those communities that the frontier of cultural and social change centered by the turn of the Century.

The coming of the railroads and the opening of the coal mines brought a whole new kind of community development. The early company towns associated with the mines and the coke manufactories have been enumerated. Each of these had a company store, a company doctor and a nucleus of housing built by the company and rented to the employees. Some employees preferred to build their own houses and save money on rent, so the companies leased land on which they could build. Schools and medical care and some other services provided by the company were ordinarily financed in this period by deductions from the miners' wages.[31]

Because of the minimal services in the company towns, Trinidad and to a lesser degree Walsenburg grew into service centers for the mining communities around them. Trinidad's growth was dramatic. From a small trading center it blossomed in a year after the railroad reached El Moro into a town of 1100 persons. By 1882 it claimed 6,000 persons and its growth continued on into the closing years of the Century.[32]

Elsewhere in these counties, small villages leveled off as ranching and farming activities reached a plateau of development. Railroads platted a townsite for virtually every main siding, but only a few of these like Timpas, La Veta and Westcliffe have survived even as small rural trading centers.[33]

In many ways the social changes were fully as dramatic as the economic developments from which they were derived. The coming of railroads and mines brought a cash economy that worked steadily to break down the patron-system of the plazas. Young men left the plazas and the ranches to work for wages in the mines or on the railroad or in the towns.[34]

When the railroads came, the Spanish speaking component of the population outnumbered all others, but the mines brought a rapid change. Several mining companies gave liquor licenses in their company towns to men who promised to serve as recruiting agents for workers. John Aeillo recruited men from Grimaldi in southern Italy. The Tarabino Brothers recruited miners from other points in Italy. John Corich recruited miners from "Austria". These were primarily from the Slavic segments of

that empire.[35] By the turn of the century, the Italian element in the
population was so large that Trinidad supported an Italian language
newspaper *La Voratore Italiano*, by 1902, shortly followed by another
journal in that language, *Corriere de Trinidad* in 1903.[36]

Detailed employment figures are available for the mines at
Walsenburg at the end of the century, giving a cross section of the
population groups involved. The three hundred miners there represented
thirteen nationalities:

    Italians 60
    Native Born Americans 47
    Negroes 45
    Japanese 32
    Slavs 21
    Mexicans 23
    English 8
    Germans 8
    Irish 7
    Welsh 4
    French 2
    Swedes 1. [37]

There remained a large enough block of Spanish speaking voters to
retain considerable political influence throughout the rest of the 19th
Century, but as newcomers became politically acculturated, the Spanish
voters position became weaker. The Spanish speaking politicians with
the highest survival rate seem to have been those that most thoroughly
adopted Anglo values of individual excellence and competition, such as
State Senator Casimiro Barela and Las Animas County Clerk, J.U. Vigil.[38]

While newspapers of the period make much of the peaceful and pro-
gressive nature of the town populations, reminiscent accounts reveal
a volatile social climate where potential violence smouldered just be-
neath the surface. One such account accuses the coal mining companies
of encouraging this tension in order to prevent effective labor organization among the miners.[39]

While the coal towns came to dominate the economic and political life of Huerfano and Las Animas counties in the long run, Custer County had its own kind of mining boom, so distinctively different that it deserves its own chapter.

NOTES ON CHAPTER V.

1. Lawrence R. Borne, "The Wootton Land and Fuel Co., 1905-1910," *Colorado Magazine*, Vol. IXLIV, #3 (1969), pp. 189-208.

2. Joel Barker, "Colorado Mail Service, 1859-1885," *Colorado Magazine*, Vol. IXLIV, #3 (1972), pp. 219-237.

3. Hugh T. Glen, "Year by Year Outline, Corporate and Physical History of the Denver and Rio Grande Western Railroad Company and its Predecessor Companies, 1870-1954," in: Lucius Beebe and Charles Clegg, *Rio Grande, Mainline of the Rockies*, Berkeley, California, Howell-North, 1962, pp. 371-380.

4. R. B. Johnson and J. G. Stephens, *Coal Resources of the La Veta Area*, Huerfano County, Colorado, U.S.G.S. Coal Investigations Map, (Washington, D.C.: USGS, 1954).

   R. B. Johnson, *Geology and Coal Resources of the Walsenburg Area*, Huerfano County, Colorado, U.S.G.S. Bulletin 1042-O, (Washington, D.C.: USGS 1958), pp.

5. R. C. Hills, *Coal Fields of Colorado: Mineral Resources of the United States of 1892*, (Washington, D.C.: USGS, 1893), pp. 324-331.

6. James Cameron, unpublished manuscript, (untitled) CWA File on Las Animas County, Colorado, Colorado Historical Society, pp. 252-255.

7. H. Lee Scamehorn, *Pioneer Steelmaker in the West*, (Boulder, Colorado: Pruett Press, 1976), pp. 10 ff.

8. Borne, *op. cit.*, pp. 189-208.

9. Cameron, *op. cit.*, pp. 253-254.

10. Eugene Frey, *Report of Investigations, Hartville Iron District, Platte County, Wyoming*, (Washington, D.C.: U.S. Bureau of Mines, 1947), pp. 2-3.

11. *ibid.*

12. Cameron, *op. cit.*, pp. 254-255.

13. Lewis Atherton, *The Cattle Kings*, (Lincoln: University of Nebraska Press, 1972), pp. 170-192.

14. Hiram Latham, *Trans-Missouri Stock Raising*, (Denver: Old West, 1972 reprint), pp. 1 ff.

   Walter, Baron von Richtofen, *Cattle Raising on the Plains of North America*, (N.Y.: Appleton, 1885), pp. 1 ff.

James S. Brisbin, *The Beef Bonanza*, (Philadelphia, Lippincott, 1881), pp. 1 ff.

15. Atherton, *op. cit.*, pp. 218-240.

   also: Gene M. Gressley, *Bankers and Cattlemen*, (Lincoln: University of Nebraska Press, 1971), pp. 243-272.

16. William B. Taylor and Elliott West, "Patron Leadership at the Crossroads: Southern Colorado in the Late 19th Century," *Pacific Historical Reviews*, Vol. 42, #3 (August, 1973), pp. 335-357.

17. *ibid.* pp. 389-408.

18. Peake, *op. cit.*, pp. 145 ff.

19. A. W. McHendrie, "Trinidad and its Environs," *Colorado Magazine*, Vol. 6, #5, (September 1929), pp. 159-170.

20. LeRoy R. Hafen, "Mexican Land Grants in Colorado," *Colorado Magazine*, Vol. 8 (1931), pp. 95-106.

21. William R. White, "Illegal Fencing on the Colorado Range," *Colorado Magazine*, Vol. 52, #1, (Spring, 1975), pp. 93-119.

22. *ibid.* pp. 105-116.

   also: Peake, *op. cit.*, 69-78.

23. Peake, *op. cit.*, pp. 272-275, and for comparison see: T.A. Larson, "The Winter of 1886-87 in Wyoming," *Annals of Wyoming*, Vol. 14, #1 (January, 1942), pp. 5-17.

24. *ibid.*,

   also: Gressley, *op. cit.*, pp. 243-272.

25. Peake, *op. cit.*, pp. 275-281.

26. J. Preston Dunleavy, unpublished manuscript in the CWA Collections for Las Animas County, Colorado Historical Society, pp. 789-790.

27. Donald A. MacKendrick, "Before the Newlands Act; State Sponsored Reclamation Projects in Colorado, 1888-1903", *Colorado Magazine*, Vol. LII, #1, (Winter, 1975), pp. 1-21.

28. *ibid.*, pp. 18-20.

29. *ibid.*, pp. 18-19.

30. *ibid.*, pp. 20-21.

31. Cameron manuscript, *op. cit.*, pp. 252-255, George G. Suggs, Jr., "The Colorado Coal Miners' Strike of 1903-04", *Journal of the West*, Vol. 7, #1, (January 1973), p. 37.

32. McHendrie, *op. cit.*, pp. 159-170.

33. Current Colorado highway map population figures, Colorado State Highway Department, 1977.

34. Taylor and West, *op. cit.*, pp. 335-357.

35. Cameron mss, *op. cit.*, pp. 252-255.

36. Newspaper list at the Colorado Historical Society Library reference room desk.

37. *Camp and Plant*, Vol. 1, #17, Saturday, April 5, 1902, pp. 265-267.

38. Taylor and West, *op. cit.*, pp. 335-357.

39. Cameron, *op. cit.*, pp. 252-255.

Chapter VI.

THE SILVER CLIFF/ROSITA HILLS MINING BOOM

Though the coal of the Raton Basin continued to be basic to the region's economy, the popular allure of precious metals brought sudden activity into one corner of the area in the 1870's. During that decade Colorado's mining magnates poured much development capital into the development of camps such as Leadville. Prospectors fanned out across the state seeking promising ore deposits that might interest such investors.

One party of prospectors examining a quartz outcrop in the Rosita Hills in 1872 found a rich concentration of silver and lead ore. They called this property the Senator lode, and worked it as an open pit to a depth of fifty to sixty feet before abandoning the claim.[1]

In 1874, other prospectors found a large deposit of copper carbonate combined with silver in the hills south of Rosita, Colorado. This was named the Humboldt-Pocohontas vein, for two principal mines that were opened upon it.[2] Estimated production for the new Rosita Hills Mining District rose from around $8,000 in 1872 to $21,986 in 1874.[3]

This was enough to attract attention, and prospectors flocked in, swelling the population of the new town of Rosita to 1,200 by 1875. Many small ore bodies came to light in the district, but lacked the individual volume that would attract a major development.[4]

Then in 1877 rich ore turned up about two miles north of Rosita. There a colorful ex-sailor named E. G. Bassick picked up samples of ore containing both gold and silver that were rich enough to induce a development group to buy a controlling interest in his claims. They named the mine the Bassick in his honor. As development work began on this property, the town of Querida, Colorado, grew up nearby.[5]

Prospectors working in the cliffs at the southern end of the White Hills found samples that assayed seventy-five per cent silver and started a rush to that area in 1878. They called their town Silver Cliff, Colorado, after one of the first mines of the new Silver Cliff Mining District.[6]

Two miles north of Silver Cliff, prospectors found an isolated deposit of rich silver ore that came to be worked as the Bull-Domingo Mine.[7]

The expanding population of these mining districts demanded county government, and in 1877, the Colorado General Assembly cut off part of then Fremont County to form Custer County, Colorado. It was named of course for the well-known Lieutenant Colonel George Armstrong Custer of the Seventh U.S. Cavalry, killed the year before on the Little Big Horn in Montana.[8]

At the peak of the boom the county's population rose to 8,080. Silver Cliff, with over 5,000 persons actively campaigned to become the capital city of Colorado.[9]

Like much of the silver ore elsewhere in Colorado, that of the Rosita Hills and the Silver Cliff districts contained both silver and lead, with varying amounts of other metals such as gold and copper. At this stage in the art of ore reduction, such ores were difficult to process efficiently. Only the highest grade of ores could be smelted directly. Fourteen mill and smelter plants were set up in the district at a cost of over a million dollars. Several of them were build around complex processing sequences, and at least one claimed a "secret" process.[10]

The freighting activity needed to support such a development

The Bassick Mine at Querida was the first major producer in the
Silver Cliff mining boom.   *Denver Public Library*

attracted the attention of the Denver and Rio Grande Railroad and that organization built a narrow gauge line up Grape Creek in the spring of 1881.[11]

Heavy investments in plant and equipment and in the extension of underground workings continued at most of the mines until 1882.[12]

The Bassick remained the largest scale producer of gold and silver in the district. From its discovery until it closed in 1885 this mine reportedly produced about $1,500,000 in the two metals combined, and paid its stockholders dividends of $425,000.[13]

One outlying mine on Oak Creek, called the Terrible, produced over three-quarters of a million dollars worth of lead.[14]

The total production of the mining districts of Custer County through the end of the year 1884 was $4,925,214. After that date, production dropped very sharply.[15]

During the peak of activity, the towns of the silver mining country in Custer County prospered from payrolls and supply contracts. Silver Cliff boasted twenty-five saloons, twenty groceries, ten blacksmith shops, eight drygoods stores, seven clothing stores, six butcher shops, six bakeries, five barbers, four hardware stores, four harness shops and thirty other business establishments of unspecified nature. There were four churches, a good water system and improved streets.[16]

Rosita and Querida remained smaller than Silver Cliff, but had substantial business development themselves.[17]

The decline of these towns quickly followed upon the closing of the major mines and mills in 1884-1885. Production of the county's mines for the next three years ran from $111,000 to $160,000 per year. Most of this came from reworking old mine dumps by hand-sorting ore.[18]

In the spring of 1888, the D. & R.G. narrow-gauge up Grape Creek washed out at many points in a single flood. The company abandoned the line at this time, since the level of mining activity did not seem to justify replacement of this difficult-to-maintain stretch of track.[19]

The cyanide process for chemically leaching gold out of low-grade ores came into widespread use in the mid 1890's. Several small cyanide plants gave brief flurries of promotional activity in the old camps, as investors hoped they could profitably re-open the mines. In fact, most of the subsequent mineral recovery operations in the Custer County mines has been limited to the reprocessing of old mine dumps to get out the last dregs of precious metals from them. After 1890 gold and silver yields seldom ranged above $40,000 in any one year, and steadily trailed off below that figure by the time of World War I.[20] Then high lead prices that continued after the war brought about the re-opening of the Terrible, which operated until a fire destroyed much of its timbering in 1928.[21]

The D. & R.G. built a standard gauge line into the area in 1901 and placed their station at Westcliffe. Many of the remaining residents at Silver Cliff moved the mile or so to Westcliffe, and the county seat of Custer County was moved to Westcliffe in 1929.[22] Since that time the former boom town, though retaining its corporate identity, has served as a "suburb" to Westcliffe's 300 population.[23]

As mining activity diminished, farming and ranching became the important remaining activity for the whole Wet Mountain valley and its continuing link to the economy of a changing region.[24]

<u>NOTES ON CHAPTER VI.</u>

1. Samuel F. Emmons, "The Mines of Custer County, Colorado," in:
   Whitman Cross (ed.) *Geology of the Silver Cliff and Rosita Hills,
   Colorado*, 17th Annual Report of the U.S. Geological Survey,
   (1896), pp. 412-413.

2. Carl Wulsten, "History of the Pocahontas Silver Mine," *The
   Great Divide*, Vol. 6, #6, (February 1892), pp. 1-4.

   see also: R. Neilson Clark, *The Humboldt-Pocahontas Vein, Rosita,
   Colorado*, (Rosita, Colorado: reprint from Vol. 7, *Transactions
   of the American Institute of Mining Engineers*, 1878), pp. 1-2.

3. Clark, *op. cit.*, pp. 5-6.

4. Emmons, *op. cit.*, pp. 412-415.

5. William Rathbun and Ed Bathke, "Bassick and His Wonderful Mine,"
   Denver Westerners' Brand Book, Vol. 20 (1964), pp. 319-349.

6. Emmons, *op. cit.*, pp. 413-414.

7. *ibid.*, p. 413.

8. LeRoy R. Hafen, "The Counties of Colorado: A History of Their
   Creation and the Origin of their Names, *Colorado Magazine*,
   March 1931, p. 56.

9. Raymond G. Colwell, "The Wet Mountain Valley, Silver Cliff and
   Westcliffe," unpublished manuscript read at the Ghost Town Club,
   October 16, 1947, copy in the Colorado Historical Society manu-
   scripts collections, Denver, pp. 3-5.

10. Emmons, *op. cit.*, pp. 416-419.

11. *Rocky Mountain News*, May 12, 1881, p. 1.

12. Emmons, *op. cit.*, pp. 416-419.

13. Emmons, *op. cit.*, pp. 430-438.

14. Charles W. Henderson, *Mining in Colorado* (Washington, D.C.:
    GPO, 1926), U.S. Geological Survey Professional Paper #138,
    pp. 112-113.

15. Emmons, *op. cit.*, p. 420.

16. *Denver Tribune*, January 1, 1881, p. 1.

17. *Rocky Mountain News*, August 9, 1874, p. 4.

18. Rathbun and Bathke, *op. cit.*, pp. 333-335.

19. Colwell, *op. cit.*, p. 21.

20. *Denver Times*, Dec. 31, 1898, pp. 19 and 30.

21. *Denver Post*, September 3, 1972, p. 8.

22. *Pueblo Sunday Chieftain*, October 24, 1965, Section C., p. 1.

23. Colwell, *op. cit.*, pp. 21-25.

24. Colwell, *op. cit.*, pp. 16-20.

Chapter VII. THE NEW CENTURY OPENS

As the last calendar pages of the Nineteenth Century came down, business and industrial interests optomistically forecast a period of rapid and accellerating growth. Not all of the predictions came true, but there was enough growth in the economy to please most promoters in Las Animas and Huerfano Counties. Custer County hoped for another mining boom, but was destined to disappointment.

Economic growth, however, had a price, and in this case the price came in the form of growing tension between mine operators and miners over wages and hours and living and working conditions in the mining communities. This tension soon erupted into the biggest news of the early 1900's and put some of the mining country's place names indelibly on the map.

As indicated earlier, there was a rapid expansion of coal mining activity at the turn of the century. Colorado Fuel and Iron Company opened the following new mines within the years immediately after 1900:

Primero - Tercio - Quatro - Morley - Tobasco - Berwyn.

The Company also set up a washer and several hundred coke ovens at Segundo, a washer and three hundred coke ovens at Tobasco, and additional mines at Walsenburg.

Some of the mines were running two ten-hour shifts each day.[1]

The mining companies continued to recruit much of their labor supply directly from overseas. The longer-established ethnic groups in the mining towns resented this practice. The defensive reaction on the part of the newcomers increased the clannishness of the Italians, Croatians and Serbians. Some residents of the mining towns felt that the companies deliberately encouraged ethnic group hatreds in order to combat labor union organization efforts.[2]

Many of the millions of tons of coal mined in the Raton Basin were
shipped north to the Colorado Fuel and Iron Mills at Pueblo.
Colorado Historical Society.

Miners earned an average of $3.00 per ten hour shift, whether they worked on an hourly or on a tonnage basis. Both systems were common in these coal mines. This was typical of what miners could expect to earn in all types of underground work throughout the west.

During this period, cowboys in the surrounding ranch country still received $30.00 per month and their board and room. In the boom-town atmosphere of the expanding coal mining towns, a construction laborer could earn up to $2.00 per day. Skilled carpenters might earn $4.00 per day when they furnished their own tools. With this pattern of wage relationships, wages themselves were not primary source of dis-contentment for the coal miner.[3]

The matter of working conditions was far more important. Under-ground mines of the period had a high accident rate, and those of the Raton Basin were as bad as any. Viewed in terms of risks, the wages do not seem so high. Mines here had pushed down around three-thousand-feet from the openings, where heat, moisture, toxic gasses and an atmosphere filled with coal dust all contributed to the potential for instant destruction or for a lingering death from respiratory troubles.[4]

Mines of this area paid their men only once a month, and paid in scrip that could be redeemed at face value at the company store or the company-licensed saloon, where prices were posted higher than those in the nearby cities. Merchants from "outside" were not permitted to deliver goods within the camps.

Deductions for services that many miners felt were inadequate came from the payrolls, whether the miners used the services or not.

Company housing was jerry-built, crammed in against the mine or the mill, and furnished at an inflated rental rate. Leases of tracts where one might build his own shack were easily revocable if a miner were fired, and no compensations were allowed for improvements on such a tract when a miner moved away. The companies did almost everything they could to avert unionization of the mines.[5]

Finally, in 1903, the miners did strike. The companies used all their local political resources to put pressure on the strikes, and evicted strikers and their families from company housing and from company-owned land. As tension flared, the mining companies advanced money to the state and the counties to pay the expenses of a military intervention along with the cost of special deputies hired to protect the trainloads of strike-breakers brought in from the Pennsylvania coal fields and elsewhere.[6]

Often billed as "indecisive," the 1903-04 strike was actually one of the most important historic events of the region. It accomplished several things: It helped, through shared misery, to break down the old barriers of communication between ethnic groups of the miners. The strike also revealed the power and the irresponsibility of the mine owners and their key employees. It proved to all the miners the need for unions. And it attracted much local sympathy for the situation of the miners among residents of the trading centers like Trinidad and Walsenburg.[7]

When the miners went back to work, the companies tightened their grip on the mining towns. They blacklisted men that they regarded as troublemakers. They blatantly interferred in the 1904 elections. They held the line on pay and services to the miners. With conditions no better than before the strike, and with more effective communication between groups of miners, tension continued to build.[8]

By 1913, the situation in the mining camps reached the boiling point. The miners went out on strike. The companies once again evicted them from the mining company towns, so the strikers and their families went into temporary camps outside of company property.

This time more widespread violence flared. The Colorado National Guard occupied the coal mining country in force. For all practical purposes constitutional processes were virtually suspended.

After a number of threats, Colorado National Guardsmen attacked a strikers' camp at Ludlow Station on April 19, 1914. The camp was destroyed and half a dozen strikers and at least thirteen women and children were killed.[9]

The incident at Ludlow caused retalitory raids by the strikers in whichthey burned down company properties throughout the district, took over the town of Trinidad and generally made preparations to better defend themselves. News of the disaster at Ludlow set off widespread reactions by labor organizations, the press and the general public across the nation and cost the companies and the National Guard much of their former public support. The raid quickly destroyed the credibility of the National Guard as a peace-keeping force for the area.

Federal troops were soon brought into the area and stayed on into 1915, and these well-disciplined regulars carefully avoided incidents, generally holding the lid on a tense situation. John D. Rockefeller, Jr., with a controlling interest in the C.F. & I. properties, personally visited the area. He came forward with a plan that was essentailly a company-union system, but one that provided for some worker representation, for grievance channels, and for compliance with the State's existing eight-hour-day law, and met most of the miners' other demands except that of union recognition.

The outbreak of World War I in Europe brought a rapid expansion of the demand for coal. There was massive production and full employment in the coal fields throughout the war years. Union organizational activities continued, but full unionization of the mines remained a long way off. The limited reforms instituted by Rockefeller served to delay active unionization and the wartime wages and employment levels alleviated some tension in the coal mining camps.[10]

Expanding coal production throughout this period brought a high level of business activity in the towns of Walsenburg and Trinidad. By this time these two places had become the focal point for the farm and ranch trade of the Raton Basin as well as mining and railroad centers. Both locally and nation-wide, the increasing industrial population through the early 1900's assured a strong market for meat, hides and wool. Prices remained high through most of the early 20th Century, and this general prosperity brought steady change to the ranch country.

Classic, unrestricted open-range grazing was a thing of the past in southern Colorado by this time. Ranchers owned most of the springs and the land along the stream courses, and thus controlled the use of intervening public lands. Working on fenced ranges, the "cowboy" spent less time chasing cows, and more time tending windmills, maintaining small irrigation ditches to water the meadows, and putting up hay for winter feed.[11]

Development of intensive irrigated farming along the Arkansas River east of Pueblo to the Kansas line had several effects on ranching in the region. The appropriation of this irrigation water did forestall what might have been more extensive upstream irrigation projects by ranchers,

but this effect was more than offset by the fact that the newly irrigated farms just outside the Raton Basin provided a feed source and
consequently the beginnings of cattle feeding operations that improved
the local market for feeder cattle from the ranches in these three
counties.[12]

Ranchers here shared in the benefits of the general price rise
caused by the depletion of herds in Montana and Wyoming through winter
losses in 1911-1912. Also, the steady expansion of population in the
mining towns brought a stronger local market for beef. The outbreak of
World War I brought rapid increases in the prices for farm and ranch
commodities. The favorable climate of the Raton Basin helped stock-
growers again in 1918-1919, when a severe drought swept the far Northern
Plains.[13]

With this steady improvement in economic conditions, the ranchers
of the Raton Basin could afford to buy new kinds of manufactured goods.
Perhaps the most important of these were automobiles and trucks, which
began to appear in the mining towns right after the turn of the century.
In 1907, the mass-produced Model T Ford became available. Initially it
sold for $500, but over the next twenty years of standardization, mass
production and sheer salesmanship pushed sales upward and prices down-
ward.

By the outbreak of World War I in 1914, the automobile and the
light truck had replaced the stagecoach on the mail routes of the Raton
Basin. Most ranchers bought cars or trucks in this same period.

The primary effect of this improved mobility was the decrease in
the isolation of ranch life. Coupled with rising prices and expanding
credit, the new ease of access to the towns encourged ranch families to
buy more consumer goods. These products replaced many of the things

that the rural population had once made for themselves, and in this way the ranchers became steadily less self-sufficient than their ancestors of the 19th Century.

Such mobility made it practicable for people to go out and homestead isolated locations in the remaining public lands.

Telephone lines during this period pushed out across the ranch country, further linking country and town.[14]

But there still remained a vast cultural gap between the ranch country of the Raton Basin and its densely packed and poorly acculturated mining communities. Ranchers took pride in their degree of independence and their pioneer heritage. The upper classes in the trading towns looked toward the cities of Colorado and of the east for social and economic models for their way of life. And the different ethnic groups of miners still maintained their own traditions, and clung to their own languages to a degree that isolated them from economic advancement and political participation.

NOTES ON CHAPTER VII.

1. Cameron mss, *op. cit.*, pp. 252-255.

2. *ibid.*, p. 253.

3. Albert Rees, "Patterns of Wages, Prices and Productivity," in: *Wages, Prices, Profits and Productivity*, (N.Y.: Columbia University 1959), pp. 11-35.

4. Colorado State Mine Inspector's *Biennial Reports 1902*, p. 5.

5. *United Mine Workers Journal*, November 11, 19, and 26, 1903. pp. 1-2 each issue.

6. George G. Suggs, Jr., "The Colorado Coal Miners' Strike, 1903-1904," *Journal of the West*, Vol. 7, #1, (January, 1973), pp. 36-52.

7. *ibid.*, pp. 51-52.

8. *ibid.*, p. 52.

9. *Senate Document 415*, 64th Congress, 1st Session (Washington, GPO, 1916) contains the entire "Final Report and Testimony of the Commission on Industrial Relations," relative the 1913-14 strike.

10. Barron B. Beshoar, *Out of the Depths*, (Denver: Colorado Labor Historical Committee, 1942) is the best overall synthesis of the 1913-1915 strike and its entire political and social context, pp. 1-251.

11. Peake, *op. cit.*, pp. 277-281.

    also: Robert G. Dunbar, "Agricultural Adjustments in Eastern Colorado in the Eighteen-Nineties," *Agricultural History*, Vol. 18 (1944), pp. 41-52.

12. Alvin T. Steinel and D.W. Working, *History of Agriculture in Colorado*, (Fort Collins: Colorado State Universtiy, 1926), pp. 240 ff.

13. Peake, *op. cit.*, pp. 280-281.

14. Carl F. Kraenzel, *The Great Plains in Transition*, (Norman: University of Oklahoma, 1955), pp. 137-149.

Chapter VIII. ON INTO THE MODERN ERA.

It is difficult to produce a really detailed synthesis of the history of so recent a period as that between the two world wars. There has been little collection, organization and sifting of the great volume of raw materials of history for this period. But it is possible to discern some major events and some general trends.

Coal mining remained the dominant economic activity in the Raton Basin from 1920-1940, but many significant changes took place. A brief, but severe industrial depression shook the country in the last half of 1921. Acting under this pressure, coal operators sought to roll back wages toward their prewar levels. The miners went out on strike in 1922, and succeeded in preventing the wage roll-back.

Coal production remained high through the rest of the 1920's, but technical change within the industry affected employment patterns. The mines of the Raton Basin were electrically lighted as early as the turn of the century, but now electricity was turned to other uses underground. Electric haulage equipment came into the larger mines at the peak of the World War I boom. In the 1920's, mines that could afford to do so mechanized their cutting and loading operations.

These changes meant that fewer ordinary "miners" were needed, but more motormen, mechanics, machine operators, along with support personnel as electricians and machinists were hired. Coincidentally, the rising level of technical skills also made the workers able to move out into other industrial jobs in such places as Denver and Pueblo.[1]

Safety standards improved, but coal mining in deep mines such as these remained a hazardous occupation. Sedimentary formations such as those that enclose coal seams are subject to sudden rock falls. The old problems of dust and gasses, with the danger of fire or explosion were still present.

Some of the older mines closed down in the 1920's, but the main change in the coal fields came in the 'Thirties. The nationwide Depression that began in the fall of 1929 reduced the demand for metallurgical coal.

As the older and less efficient mines closed down, miners abandoned such company towns as Primero and the companies sold the buildings for salvage. Old plant equipment went into scrap metal markets during the mid Thirties when there was widespread unemployment and low labor costs, coupled with a rising overseas market for heavy metal scrap.

By the mid-1930's only Sopris, Morley, Valdez, Delagua, Jewell and Dick mines were still open in the Trinidad area, and only the Cameron, the Kebler #1, the Maitland and the Ravenwood mines were open in Huerfano County.[2]

The United Mine Workers of America organized the workers in the mines of the Raton Basin in 1934. C.F. & I. and the other mining companies recognized the union. The National Labor Relations Act of 1935 strengthened to bargaining position of the union. Under the new contracts, miners received $4.70 per day.

Both the state and the federal government enforced their health and safety standards for the coal mines more effectively from the 1930's onward.

As employment in mining declined, many miners left the district to seek employment elsewhere. Those who remained, protected by their greater union strength, became more politically active. To a large degree their support increased the strength of the Democratic party in the Raton Basin.[3]

Most citizens of the region accepted the greater political strength of the working men as a fact of life brought on by changing times. A few citizens, however sought relief for their dissatisfaction by supporting the Ku Klux Klan. By 1925, this organization had spread westward from Georgia and achieved a considerable following in Denver, Colorado. Few details of its activities in Southern Colorado are available, but it is reported to have had a branch in Trinidad, where it played on ethnic and religious hatreds of some Anglo-American Protestants.[4]

Helping to offset such reactionary forces as the Klan were important changes in education. Public schools replaced company schools in the mining country, and attendance at the public schools did much to break down the communications barriers between ethnic groups. Federally sponsored employment programs in the 1930's, such as the Civilian Conservation Corps, the Works Projects Administration, the Civil Works Administration and others helped to do the same thing for adults.

Economic and social change were not limited to the mining towns. Ranchers and farmers of the Raton Basin were affected even more sharply by the 1921 recession than industry was. Wheat prices dropped in a six month period from over $2.00 per bushel to around 50¢. Beef, mutton, wool and hides all declined in price proportionately.

Foreclosures, resulting in a substantial consolidation of holdings, characterized the financial situation of the ranchers throughout the period from 1921 to the late 1930's. Prices remained low until 1940, with the very lowest levels coming in 1934-35.[5]

There was a wave of additional homesteading on the public lands in the 1920's. Much of this, here as well as in other regions, was the use of homestead laws to help family members to acquire tracts that could round out existing holdings. The drastic revision of public land policies in 1934 brought most of the remaining public domain in the Raton Basin into managed grazing systems under the Taylor Grazing Act.

The Southeastern portion of the Raton Basin in Las Animas County lay along the edge of the "Dust Bowl," and many farm and ranch units were abandoned in the mid 1930's. Under the terms of the Bankhead-Jones Act, the Federal government bought up many marginal farms and ranches. Some of these were sold to neighboring ranchers to create more viable operating units. The remaining lands that were purchased by the government were managed as grazing units. In the years following World War II, these federal holdings were combined as part of the adjacent Comanche National Grasslands under U.S. Forest Service administration.[6]

The Twenties and Thirties brought faster and more reliable automobiles and trucks to the region. Coloradans joined in a nation-wide clamor for better roads. One might think of the Twenties as the graveled-highway era. In good weather, one could cover in an hour the distance that a covered wagon would have required in three days to traverse.

The main framework of the highway network through the Raton Basin was hard-surfaced in the 1930's when both the State and the Federal government allocated more money for highway construction due to continued public demand for better roads. U.S. Highway 85 became the major north/ south route through the region, and provided a direct route to Denver, as well as a good road over Raton Pass into New Mexico. U.S. 160 carried traffic over the mountains into the San Luis Valley. A network of state highways like Highway 12, Highway 111, and Highway 69 opened up the mountain valleys to motor traffic.

The expansion of good roads brought tourist traffic from an increasing radius, and tourist services became an important new area of economic activity in the towns of the Raton Basin.[7]

The D. & R.G. Railroad abandoned its line into the Wet Mountain Valley in 1939 after mining failed to revive in that area and after motor trucks began to handle most of the freighting needs of the ranches of that area.[8]

During the late 1930's, off across northern Colorado crept the first diesel powered locomotives of the Burlington. They had drastic long range implications for this area, for soon the diesels would replace steam locomotives on nearly the all the railroads. As this happened, the demand for coal dropped and still more mines closed.[9]

Radio reached out across the miles from Denver and Pueblo in the 1930's and brought the ranchers and miners alike into closer touch with the urban world. Working with the other forces mentioned above, radio unquestionably helped to steadily erode some of the barriers between cultural groups.[10]

By 1940, the Raton Basin was no longer a frontier in the sense of linear boundaries between cultural groups. All of the ethnic, economic, and social elements in the area had by this time developed strong ties to national institutions in business, society and government. The stage was now set for the pressures of World War II to speed up the "melting pot" process that had in reality been going on, if slowly at times, since the arrival of the first explorers and traders among the Indians of the region so very long ago. All elements in the population of the Raton Basin in 1940 could look back with pride on the work of their

predecessors in building a complex and productive society in this part
of Colorado.

NOTES ON CHAPTER VIII.

1. Beshoar, *op. cit.*, pp. 271 ff.

   also: *Coal Age* magazine in this period has in every issue detailed reports on the introduction of new machinery into the mines.

2. Cameron manuscript *op. cit.*, pp. 252-255.

3. Beshoar, *op. cit.*, pp. 361-370.

4. Gerald Lynn Marriner, "Klan Politics in Colorado," *Journal of the West*, Vol. 15, #1, Janaury 1976, pp. 76-101.

5. Kraenzel, *op. cit.*, pp. 149-164.

   also: Joseph G. Rayback, A *History of American Labor*, (N.Y.: MacMillan, 1959), pp. 290-325.

6. Sanford A. Mosk, "Land Policy and Stock Raising in the Western United States," *Agricultural History*, Vol. 17 (1943), pp. 14-30.

7. Frederic L. Paxson, "The Highway Movement, 1916-1935," *American Historical Review*, Vol. 51, (1945-46), pp. 236-253.

   and: Harry Hansen (ed.) *Colorado, A Guide to the Highest State*, (N.Y.: Hastings House, 1970), pp. 337-345.

   LeRoy R. Hafen, "The Coming of the Automobile and Improved Roads to Colorado," *Colorado Magazine*, Vol. 8, #1, 1931, pp. 1-17.

8. Colwell, *op. cit.*, p. 24.

9. Richard C. Overton, *Burlington Route*, (N.Y.: Knopf, 1965), pp. 397-406.

10. Kraenzel, *op. cit.*, pp. 232-249.

BIBLIOGRAPHY

PRIMARY SOURCES

Manuscripts

Cameron, James. MSS (untitled), pp. 252-255, CWA Interviews, Las Animas County, Colorado at the Colorado Historical Society, Denver.

Canon, Benton. MSS, "The History of the Georgia Colony," Document 363/1 CWA Interviews, Huerfano County, Colorado at the Colorado Historical Society, Denver.

Colwell, Raymond Gardner. MSS "The Wet Mountain Valley, Silver Cliff and Westcliffe," Colorado Historical Society, Denver.

Dunleavy, J. Preston. MSS (untitled), pp. 789-790, CWA Interviews, Las Animas County, at the Colorado Historical Society, Denver.

Figge, M. Bertha. MSS, "The Pocahontas/Humboldt Mines History," Western History Collections, Pueblo Regional Library.

_____. MSS, "The History of Custer County," Western History Collections of the Pueblo Regional Library.

Richeson, A.K. MSS, "Senator J.M. Madrid, Trinidad, Colorado," Document 359/6, CWA Interviews for Las Animas County, Colorado at the Colorado Historical Society.

Sporeleder, L.D. MSS, "The Georgia Colony," Document 363/1, CWA Interviews for Huerfano County, Colorado at the Colorado Historical Society.

Printed Documents

Colorado State Mine Inspector. *Biennial Report for 1902.*

Dayton, W.A., *et. al. Range Plant Handbook.* Washington, D.C.: U.S. Department of Agriculture, 1937.

Frey, Eugene. *Report of Investigations, Hartville Iron District.* Washington, D.C.: U.S. Bureau of Mines, 1947.

Goddard, E.N. and T.S. Lovering. *Geology and Ore Deposits of the Front Range, Colorado.* Washington, D.C.: U.S. Geological Survey, 1950.

Henderson, C.W.: *Mining in Colorado, a History of Discovery, Development and Production,* U.S. Geological Survey Professional Paper #138. Washington, D.C.: GAP, 1926.

Hills, R.C. *Coal Fields of Colorado.* Washington, D.C.: U.S. Geological Survey, 1893.

_____. *Spanish Peaks, Colorado, Geological Folio.* Washington, D.C.: U.S. Geological Survey, 1901.

_____. *Walsenburg, Colorado, Geologic Folio.* Washington, D.C.: U.S. Geological Survey, 1900.

Johnson, R.B. and J.G. Stephens. *Coal Resources of the La Veta Area, Huerfano County, Colorado,* Washington, D.C.: U.S. Geological Survey, 1954.

_____. *Geology and Coal Resources of the Walsenburg Area, Huerfano County, Colorado.* U.S.G.S. Bulletin 1042-0. Washington, D.C.: GPO, 1958.

McLaughlin, T.G. *Ground Water in Huerfano County, Colorado.* U.S.G.S. Water Supply Paper #1805. Washington, D.C.: GPO, 1966.

Parker, R.L. and Hildebrand, F.A. *Preliminary Report on Alkalic Intrusive Rocks in the Northern Wet Mountains, Colorado.* U.S.G.S. Professional Paper #450. Washington, D.C.: 1961.

U.S. Department of Agriculture, *Climate and Man, The 1941 Yearbook of Agriculture,* Washington, D.C.: GPO, 1941.

U.S. Congress. "An Act to Confirm Certain Private Land Claims in the Territory of New Mexico," *U.S. Statutes at Large,* Vol. 12 (1859-63), Washington, D.C. 1864.

U.S. Congress. *House Report 195.* 36th Congress, 1st Session, 1860.

U.S. Congress. *Senate Report 228.* 36th Congress, 1st Session, 1860.

Wood, G.H., *et. al. Geology and Coal Resources of the Gulnare, Cuchara Pass and Stonewall Area, Huerfano and Las Animas Counties, Colorado.* Washington, D.C.: U.S.G.S., 1956.

SECONDARY SOURCES

Books

Aguilar, Jose de Onis. *Hispanic Contributions to the State of Colorado*. Denver: n.p. 1976.

Alter, Cecil J. *Jim Bridger*. Norman: University of Oklahoma Press, 1962.

Athearn, Robert G. *Rebel of the Rockies*. New Haven: Yale University Press, 1962.

_____. *High Country Empire*. Lincoln: University of Nebraska Press, 1960.

Atherton, Lewis. *The Cattle Kings*. Lincoln: University of Nebraska Press, 1972.

Beckner, Raymond M. *Along Colorado Trails*. Pueblo, Colorado: O'Brien Printing and Stationery, 1975.

_____. *Old Forts of Southern Colorado*. Pueblo, Colorado: O'Brien Printing and Stationery, 1975.

Beebe, Lucius and Charles Clegg. *Rio Grande, Mainline of the Rockies*. Berkeley, California: Howell/North, 1962.

Berthrong, Donald J. *The Southern Cheyennes*. Norman: University of Oklahoma Press, 1968.

Beshoar, Barron B. *Out of the Depths*. Denver: Colorado Labor Historical Committee, 1942.

Bolton, Herbert E. (ed.) *Spanish Explorations in the Southwest*. N.Y.: 1916.

Brebner, John B. *Explorers of North America*. N.Y.: Doubleday, 1955.

Brisbin, James S. *The Beef Bonanza*. Philadelphia: Lippincott, 1881.

Canfield, John G. *Mines and Mining Men of Colorado*. Denver: Canfield, 1893.

Carter, Harvey L. *Dear Old Kit*. Norman: University of Oklahoma Press, 1968.

Delaney, Howard L. *All Our Yesterdays*. Walsenburg, Colorado: Consolidated Publishing Co., 1914.

Emmitt, Robert. *The Last War Trail*. Norman: University of Oklahoma Press, 1958.

Fehrenback, T.R. *Comanches, The Destruction of a People*. N.Y.: Knopf, 1974.

Flint, R.F. *Glacial and Pleistocene Geology*. N.Y.: John Wiley, 1957.

Forbes, Jack D. *Apache, Navaho and Spaniard*. Norman: University of Oklahoma Press, 1960.

Fowler, Jacob. (Elliott Couse, ed.) *The Journal of Jacob Fowler*. N.Y.: F.P. Harper, 1898.

Gregg, Josiah. *Commerce of the Prairies*. Philadelphia: Lippincott, 1962.

Gressley, Gene M. *Bankers and Cattlemen*. Lincoln: University of Nebraska Press, 1971.

Hafen, LeRoy R. and Frncis M. Young. *Fort Laramie and the Pageant of the West*. Glendale: Arthur H. Clark Co. 1940.

Haley, J. Evetts. *Charles Goodnight*. Boston: Houghton-Mifflin, 1936.

Hansen, Harry (ed.) *Colorado, A Guide...* N.Y.: Hastings, 1970.

Hoig, Stan. *Sand Creek Massacre*. Norman: Oklahoma University Press, 1963.

Hyde, George E. *Indians of the High Plains*. Norman: University of Oklahoma Press, 1959.

Jablow, Joseph. *The Cheyenne in Plains Indian Trade Relations*. Locust Valley, M.Y.: J.J. Augustin, 1951.

James, Edwin (compiler). *Account of an Expedition from Pittsburg to the Rocky Mountains*. Philadelphia: Carey and Lee, 1823.

Keats, John. *Eminent Domain*. N.Y.: Charterhouse, 1973.

Kraenzel, Carl F. *The Great Plains in Transition*. Norman: University of Oklahoma Press, 1955.

Lavender, David. *Bent's Old Fort*. N.Y.: Doubleday, 1954.

MacGowan, Kenneth and Joseph A. Hester, Jr. *Early Man in the New World*. N.Y.: Doubleday, 1962.

Nastir, Abraham P. *Before Lewis and Clark*. St. Louis: Historical Documents Foundation, 1952.

Oliva, Leo E. *Soldiers on the Santa Fe Trail*. Norman: University of Oklahoma Press, 1961.

Overton, Richard C. *Burlington Route*. N.Y.: Knopf, 1965.

Owens, Robert P. *Huerfano Valley as I Knew It.* Canon City: Master Printers, 1975.

Peake, Ora B. *The Colorado Range Cattle Industry.* Glendale: Arthur H. Clark Co., 1937.

Pearson, Jim B. *The Maxwell Land Grant.* Norman: University of Oklahoma Press, 1961.

Phillips, Paul C. *The Fur Trade.* Norman: University of Oklahoma Press, 1961.

Pike, Zebulon. *Sources of the Mississippi and the Western Louisiana Territory.* Ann Arbor, Michigan: University Microfilm Reprint, 1966.

Richtofen, Walter, Baron von. *Cattle Raising on the Plains of North America.* N.Y.: Appleton, 1885.

Riddle, Kenyon. *Records and Maps of the Old Santa Fe Trail.* Raton, New Mexico: n.p. 1949.

Roe, Frank G. *The Indian and the Horse.* Norman: University of Oklahoma Press, 1955.

Scamehorn, H. Lee. *Pioneer Steelmaker in the West.* Boulder Colorado: Pruett Press, 1976.

Secoy, Frank R. *Changing Military Patterns on the Great Plains.* Locust Valley, N.Y.: J.J. Augustin, 1953.

Seeley, Charles L. *Pioneer Days in the Arkansas Valley of Southern Colorado.* Denver: Seeley, 1932.

Sporleder, Louis B. *The Romance of the Spanish Peaks.* Pueblo: O'Brien, 1960.

Sprague, Marshall. *The Great Gates.* Boston: Little, Brown & Co., 1964.

Steinel, Alvin T. and D.W. Working. *History of Agriculture in Colorado.* Fort Collins: Colorado State University, 1926.

Taylor, Morris F. *First Mail West.* Albuquerque: University of New Mexico Press, 1971.

Thomas, A.B. *After Coronado.* Norman: University of Oklahoma Press, 1935.

_____. *Plains Indians and New Mexico.* Albuquerque: University of New Mexico Press, 1940.

Turk, Gayle. *Wet Mountain Valley.* Colorado Springs: Little London Press, 1975.

Twitchell, Ralph E. (compiler) *Spanish Archives of New Mexico*. Cedar Rapids: Torch Press, 1914.

Ubbelohde, Carl (ed.) A *Colorado Reader*. Boulder: Pruett Press, 1964.

Vroom, James W. *The Las Animas Land Grant*. Akron, Ohio: Capron and Curtice, 1893.

Weber, William A. "Plant Geography in the Southern Rocky Mountains," in: H.E. Wright (ed.). *The Quaternary of the United States*. Princeton: Princeton University Press, 1965.

Wood, Richard G. *Stephen Harriman Long*. Glendale: Arthur H. Clark Co., 1966.

Pamphlets

Anon., *Annual Directory of Custer County, Colorado*. Silver Cliff, Colorado: Prospect/News, 1880.

Clark, R. Neilson. *The Humboldt/Pocahontas Vein*. Rosita, Colorado: n.p. 1878.

Latham, Hiram. *Trans-Missouri Stock Raising*. Denver: Old West, 1972.

Matthews, Albert. *The Purgatory River of Colorado*. Cambridge, Massachusetts: Wilson, 1902.

Mieir, William O. *Westcliffe, Colorado*. Denver: Carson/Harper, 1898.

Anon. *Prospectus of the Robinson Hill Consolidated Mining Co. of Custer County, Colorado*. Denver, Collier and Cleaveland, 1881.

Newspapers

Colorado Chieftain, May 13, 1874. "Huerfano County."

Pueblo Sunday Chieftain, October 24, 1965. Section C. p. 1.

Pueblo Chieftain, August 10, 1969, p. 1. x. "Augilar".

Pueblo Star Journal and Sunday Chieftain, February 24, 1968, "Bassick at Querida..."

Denver Post, September 3, 1972, p. 8.

Denver, *Tribune*, January 1, 1881, p. 1.

Denver Times, December 31, 1898, pp. 19 and 30.

La Junta Tribune, December 15, 1933. "John W. Prowers..."

Rocky Mountain News, August 9, 1874, p. 4.

Rocky Mountain News, May 12, 1881, p. 1.

Rocky Mountain News, Festival Edition, August 30, 1970, p. 8.

Articles

Adams, Blanche V. "The Second Colorado Cavalry in the Civil War."
     Colorado Magazine. Vol. 8, 1931, pp. 95-106.

Agogino, George A., "The Paleo Indian in North America," *Genus*,
     Vol. 19, 1-4, 1963, pp. 3-17.

Arnold, Samuel P. "William Bent." *Mountain Men and the Fur Trade.*
     Glendale: Arthur H. Clark Co., 1968, Vol. 6, pp. 61-84.

Barker, Joel. "Colorado Mail Service, 1859-1885." *Colorado Magazine*,
     Vol. 44, 3, 1972, pp. 219-237.

Borne, Lawrence R. "The Wootton Land and Fuel Co." *Colorado Magazine*,
     Vol. 40, 3, 1969, pp. 189-208.

Bradfute, Richard W. "The Las Animas Land Grant." *Colorado Magazine*,
     Vol. 41, 1 1970, pp. 26-43.

Carter, Harvey L. "Dick Wootton," *Mountain Men and the Fur Trade.*
     Glendale: Arthur H. Clark Co. 1966, Vol. 3, pp. 407-411.

Cheatham, Francis T., "Early Settlements of Southern Colorado,"
     Colorado Magazine, Vol. (1928), pp. 1-8.

Covington, James W. "Federal Relations with the Colorado Utes, 1861-
     1865." *Colorado Magazine*, Vol. 28, 1961, pp. 257-266.

Cox, Isaac J. "Exploration of the Louisiana Frontier," *American
     Historical Review*, 1904, pp. 152 ff.

Emmons, Samuel F. "Some Mines of Rosita and Silver Cliff," *Trans-
     actions of the American Institute of Mining Engineers*, Vol. 26,
     1926, print.

Hafen, LeRoy R. "Colorado Mountain Men," *Colorado Magazine*, Vol. 30.
     1953, pp. 14-28.

_____, "Coming of the Automobile and Improved Roads to
     Colorado," *Colorado Magazine*, Vol. 8, 1931, pp. 1-17.

_____, "Counties of Colorado." *Colorado Magzine*, Vol. 8,
     1931.

_____, "Mexican Land Grants in Colorado," *Colorado Magazine*,
     Vol. 4, 1927, pp. 81-93.

Haley, J. Evetts, "The Comanchero Trade," *Southwestern Historical Quarterly*, Vol. 38, 1834-35, pp. 157-176.

Kroeber, Alfred L. "The Arapaho." *Bulletin of the American Museum of Natural History*, Vol. 18, 1902, pp. 1 ff.

Larson, T.A. "The Winter of 1886-87 in Wyoming," *Annals of Wyoming*, Vol. 14, 1, 1942, pp. 5-17.

LeCompte, Janet, "Charles Autobees," *Mountain Men and the Fur Trade*. Glendale: Arthur H. Clark Co. 1966, Vol. 4, p. 37.

_____. "Matthew Kinkead," *Mountain Men and the Fur Trade*, Glendale: Arthur H. Clark Co., 1966, Vol. 2, pp. 188-199.

_____. "Maurice LeDuc," *Mountain Men and the Fur Trade*, Glendale: Arthur H. Clark Co., 1968, Vol. 6, pp. 227-240.

_____. "Simeon Turley," *Mountain Men and the Fur Trade*, Glendale: Arthur H. Clark Co., 1969, Vol. 7, pp. 302-303.

Mahan, Bill, "The Telegraph in Southern Colorado, 1867-1881," *San Luis Valley Historian*, Vol. 7, 1965, pp. 4-12.

Marriner, Gerald L. "Klan Politics in Colorado," *Journal of The West*, Vol. 15, 1976, pp. 76-101.

MacKendrick, Donald A. "Before the Newlands Act." *Colorado Magazine*, Vol. 52, 1975, pp. 1-21.

McKendrie, A.W. "Origin of the Name of the Purgatoire River." *Colorado Magazine*, Vol. 5, 1928, pp. 18-22.

Mosk, Sanford A. "Land Policy and Stock Raising in the Western United States," *Agricultural History*, Vol. 17, 1943, pp. 14-30.

Murray, Robert A. "Fur Trade of the Fort Laramie Region." *Museum of the Fur Trade Quarterly*, Vol. 3, 1967, pp. 1-4.

Pappas, Peter J. "100 Years of the Wet Mountain Valley," *Auraria Transcript* January 28, 1976.

Paxon, Frederic L. "The Highway Movement, 1916-1935." *American Historical Review*, Vol. 51, 1946, pp. 236-253.

Oster, John E., "Diplomatic and Treaty Relations Between the United States and Mexico," *Hispanic American Historical Review*, Vol. 7. 1927, pp. 2-24.

Rees, Albert, "Patterns of Wages, Prices and Productivity," in: *Wages, Prices, Profits and Productivity*, N.Y.: Columbia University, 1959, pp. 11-35.

Renaud, E.B. "Indians of Colorado." in: *Colorado: Short Studies of its Past and Present*, Boulder: University of Colorado, 1927.

Russell, Carl P. "Wilderness Rendezvous Period of the American Fur Trade." *Oregon Historical Quarterly*, Vol. 42, 1941, pp. 1-47.

Savage, William W., Jr. "Stockmen's Associations and the Range Cattle Industry," *Journal of the West*, Vol. 14, 1975, pp. 52-59.

Stevens, F.F., "Missouri and the Santa Fe Trade," *Missouri Historical Review*, Vol. 10, 1916, pp. 233-262.

Suggs, George G., Jr., "The Colorado Coal Miners' Strike, 1903-04," *Journal of the West*, Vol. 7, 1973, pp. 36-52.

Taylor, Morris F., "Confederate Guerillas in Southern Colorado," *Colorado Magazine*, Vol. 46, 1969, pp. 304-323.

_____, "Captain William Craig and the Vigil and St. Vrain Land Grant," *Colorado Magazine*, Vol. 45, 1968, p. 319.

_____, "The Maxwell Cattle Co." *New Mexico Historical Review*, Vol. 49, 1974, pp. 289-324.

_____, "Ranching on the Out Boundaries of the Las Animas Grant," *Arizona and the West*, Vol. 16, 1974, p. 125-140.

Taylor, William B. and Elliott West, "Patron Leadership at the Crossroads," *Pacific Historical Review*, Vol. 42, 3, 1973, pp. 335-357.

Thomas, Chauncey, "The Spanish Fort in Colorado, 1819," *Colorado Magazine*, Vol. 14, 1937, pp. 81-85.

Edgely W. Todd, "Antonio Montero," *Mountain Men and the Fur Trade*, Glendale: Arthur H. Clark Co., 1966, Vol. 6, pp. 101-107.

Vaille, Howard T. "Early Years of the Telephone in Colorado," *Colorado Magazine*, Vol. 4, 1928, pp. 121-133.

White, William P. "Illegal Fencing on the Colorado Range," *Colorado Magazine*, Vol. 52, 1975, pp. 93-119.

Wulsten, Carl. "History of the Pocahontas Silver Mine," *The Great Divide*, Vol. 6, 1892, pp. 1-4.

Theses

Blankenship, Warren M. "The Hardscrabble Mining District," Denver
    University, 1959, MA Thesis.

Hall, Clifford C. "Wagon Roads in Colorado," Boulder: University
    of Colorado, 1946, MA Thesis.

Smith, H.D. "Early Life in Trinidad and the Purgatory Valley,"
    Boulder: University of Colorado, 1930, MA Thesis.

ABOUT THE AUTHOR

Robert A. Murray was born in Craig, Nebraska, and has lived in the West since 1957. He attended Nebraska State Teachers College at Wayne, where he received his A.B. in history and geography; Kansas State University, where he was granted an M.S. in history and government. Since that time he has performed additional graduate study at Eastern Montana College, the University of Northern Colorado, the University of Wyoming, and California Western University. For some years a public school teacher, he served as a historian with the U.S. National Park Service from 1958-1968, and since that time has been head of a consulting firm, Western Interpretive Services, Inc., specializing in historical research and interpretive planning. In addition to this study, he has had published sixteen books and major monographs, numerous articles in scholarly journals and has been a frequent guest lecturer at institutions of higher learning in the West.

www.ingramcontent.com/pod-product-compliance
Lightning Source LLC
Chambersburg PA
CBHW081219280526
45787CB00006B/2448